On the Path
to *Enlightenment*

A Hope for Humanity

Chris Hamilton

BALBOA
PRESS

A DIVISION OF HAY HOUSE

Balboa Press books may be ordered through booksellers or by contacting:

Balboa Press
A Division of Hay House
1663 Liberty Drive
Bloomington, IN 47403
www.balboapress.com.au
1-(877) 407-4847

ISBN: 978-1-4525-1175-7 (sc)
ISBN: 978-1-4525-1176-4 (e)

Balboa Press rev. date: 10/09/2013

*I dedicate this book
to the loving spirit
who came into this life
as my daughter, Andrea.*

Contents

INTRODUCTION

I HAVE ALWAYS BELIEVED WE were born into this world for a purpose. I never really could accept that death was the end of life. I always felt there was more to life than being born, eating, procreating and dying. I lived, what I believe, was a fairly sheltered life. That is, until I reached my forty-third year.

I hope to show readers that there is a purpose to life, and that is the lessons we are learning in our everyday lives that give our life this purpose. I also sense that something is happening to the planet at the present time, and we are privileged to be here. There is a gradual awakening among humanity which is speeding up as time escalates around us. As more and more people take an interest in matters which are "not of this world", the purposes of our true existence will come more into focus.

I do not believe that the existence of an afterlife has anything to do with religion. I believe it is simply a fact! Somewhere in my early thirties, I began to discover philosophy, and read as much as I could find on the shelves of the library. Later, after a tragedy that shook my life wide open, I found an interest in metaphysics, and spiritual topics. I would sometimes pray, little "arrow prayers" straight from the heart. When I think about it now, I suppose I always believed in prayer. I believe our very thoughts are like a prayer when sent heavenward. Divine help is available when we ask. Our guides in the spiritual realms are ever-ready to help us and we only have to listen for the answers.

I have received what I believe is divine guidance over a period of time, and some of this guidance is channelled to uplift me in times of sadness, doubt or frustration. There have been many occasions where I have received this help.

I feel it has been given, not for me, alone, but for everyone.

If you can relate to this guidance, then it is for you. I believe the time for enlightenment and upliftment of the human race is at hand. We are being guided and helped in many ways that have not previously been open to us.

The time of awakening has come for the earth, and we are privileged to be here to experience the changes that are occurring.

The opening of humanity begins with each and every one of us. It begins when we allow ourselves to feel the pain, with acceptance; when we question our reasons for existence; when we allow ourselves just to *be*; when we open our hearts and minds into the love that is within each and every one of us. This is the way to finding enlightenment; and thereby our freedom. By walking away from the need for attachment, and the need to judge, we allow ourselves and others just to be who they are in their own perfect uniqueness.

We were born to experience life in all its many facets: to find love and to live that love. This is the path to follow.

Ever since time began, man has wondered about his existence. Why is he here? What does the future hold? Is there life after death? These; and many other questions; have plagued humankind for centuries. The world's greatest philosophers have searched for answers, yet many of their questions remain unanswered. Only those few chosen ones throughout the ages, have been able to offer answers to these questions. The answers have been hidden from the general populace for centuries. In this present age, more people are being given the opportunity to find answers to their deepest questions.

The way has been opened.

May some of your deepest yearnings be answered.

Chris Hamilton

Chapter 1

WHY WERE WE BORN?

MY DAUGHTER WAS A CATALYST in my life. She was dogmatic, argumentative, and stubborn in many ways, but she helped open me up to different views of life. I was pretty much a dreamer, and not too involved in life in general. It was her death in November 1990 that shook me into a reality I hadn't wanted to face; one that I would never have wished for in my wildest dreams. But it was a reality that is far beyond the physical world of the senses. It is a reality that smacks of the spiritual world; and the forces therein. It does not pertain to this world of materialism, as it is now, yet the two interact, and there is no way to differentiate them. I felt, no, I knew, there was more to this life than just this physical reality.

I find it sad when I hear some people say this life is all there is, and at the end there is death, the closing of a blind, nought but blackness, nothingness, a void. I cannot, and never could, accept that death would be the end of life. I guess I never really thought about it very much, but I certainly didn't think there was nothing after this life. A loving Creator could not have created us by chance; for no reason but to live and die into nothingness.

If we take a look at nature, we see the birth and death of the seasons; the birth of plant life, its death, and then it springing back to life as each new season dawns. If we look at the trees and plants, for example, as each tree dies; a little seed falls, and

1

in time; a new tree shoots up out of the fertile soil. Within each little seed is the making of a new plant, tree, or flower. Evolution continues in nature; as indeed it does in the animal and human kingdom. Our souls are continually evolving; as surely as life continues in the great universe. Each moment new planets are continually spinning, evolving, and being birthed. Nothing that exists came into being without purpose. Every experience in life has a continual spiral of purpose. We are told by spiritual philosophies that nothing happens by chance.

Our rational mind looks "out there" for an answer. Our inner self sees everything as being part of self. In Deepak Chopra's book *The Way of the Wizard,* he gives us an explanation for the order of life:

"Energy and information are basic to everything we see, hear or touch in the relevant world. Yet their primordial state is formless. A bundle of energy can drift away in a chaotic swirl like a puff of smoke; information can break down into random blips of data. It takes another force to organise the wondrous order of life—intelligence. Intelligence is the glue of the universe."

Intelligence has created life for a purpose. I believe we are born into this world to learn to evolve spiritually into our true nature. Every experience we have, we learn from in some way. We are all part of the intelligence that is called God. There are many names that are used to describe this intelligence: God, Source, Universal energy, the universe, the All-That-Is and many others. Whatever you call this oneness with Source, it matters not. We are all part of it. We are as much a part of this Source as any other human being or, in fact, any part of nature or the planet, or the universes themselves. Everything that exists is God. There is nothing that is not God. You may find this hard to accept if you were brought up with a religious background, seeing God as a separate being sitting on a throne in heaven, but the great masters throughout time have told us that all life is experience of God Source.

Before we come into this physical dimension we are and always have been spirit. Our souls have always existed as part of the creative force. They were before the beginning of the world, and will be still when the world has passed away. We are far more than our physical bodies. We are told we have lived many, many lives, and each time we die in the physical sense; we are given an opportunity to view our past mistakes. We see what we failed to do; or how we may have hurt someone; or infringed on their free-will through trying to control them or bend them to our ways. Sometimes failing to do something is the greater error. To make amends for these past "mistakes" we are given an opportunity to be born into circumstances that allow us the chance to alleviate our wrongs and so give our soul another chance to grow into its true oneness with itself. The circumstances we are born into; reflect the amount of learning we have completed in life.

It is our soul's choice when we choose our particular circumstances. If we are far enough along the path in our learning, we are given the privilege of choosing our parents and circumstances in order to advance further in our soul's learning. Most of the events in our life pattern are planned before we are born into the human body of a baby. Many of the circumstances which happen to us in our lifetime do not happen randomly, but are actually part of our soul's planning, and they are chosen for our greater learning, prior to our being born. We have choices along the way, but the main shape of our life pattern is not altered to a great extent by these choices. Our guides and spirit helpers are always prompting us to follow certain patterns at different junctures in our lives.

Our choices and circumstances are our responsibility. It is we who choose the hard lessons in life or the easy ones. Those who face the toughest times are often facing the greatest growth. Those who face loss of children, for example, or adverse circumstances like unhappy marriages or broken families; have, on a soul level, actually chosen these circumstances for their own chance to grow. No lesson in life is ever wasted.

Deep within our own being; we will find the answer to why we chose our particular circumstances or situations. The law of cause and effect exists in the universe. It is an immutable law that cannot be altered one iota except through the grace of God. You may have asked yourself why there seems to be so much unfairness in the world. Why are some born to rich and healthy parents and some are born deformed, or to poor parents, with seemingly little or no opportunities in life? The answer can only lie in the law of karma, or cause and effect. Many who are born into deformed bodies; are learning their soul lessons faster than most. They have chosen that pathway in life in order to speed up their soul's progress and eliminate many of the mistakes they may have made throughout their lifetimes.

We are immortal beings with many chances to achieve what would be impossible to achieve in one lifetime! Life is an ongoing cycle, always spiralling upwards towards our further growth. If we turn down opportunities for growth; or diverge from our chosen pathway, we will inevitably have as many lifetimes as we need in order to advance. But do we really want to come back time and again to learn the same lessons? It would be like staying down in class because we hadn't learnt our lesson and hadn't advanced a grade.

We often fight our circumstances, wanting to alter them. But the lesson is always waiting to be learned. If we refuse to learn it, it will rebound on us again and again in various forms until we do learn it. The way we learn is by loving and accepting all that comes to us in life unconditionally, by loving and accepting ourselves, and by loving and serving our fellowman. Whatever we are given to do in life, we should do it with total acceptance and love. This is the quickest way to learn our life's lesson. It is the way back to what every soul ultimately seeks—the way back to the God-head.

The reason we appear to be separated from our God-source here on earth; is to learn our lessons, and take them all back to Source at the end of our sojourn. We never lose our own particular personality aspect, yet we become a part of the whole at the same time. Nothing of our personality is ever lost. It just merges into the oneness called God. We have to learn to integrate our lower natures with our higher natures. To do this, it helps if we go within, to our very depths, and ask our Higher Power, or Higher Self, or God Self, whichever name we choose to call it, if we are taking the right step. We will always get back an answer if we listen for it. It may not always come in the form we expect, so it is better not to have expectations. Just ask quietly, and be open to whatever answer comes.

We are given free-will on this planet in order to understand, eventually, that the only thing we seek is the will of our God-Source. It is by trial and error we learn the lessons in life and; like the prodigal son, trying to find happiness outside of his home; we eventually learn that the very thing we seek; namely the love of our Creator-Source, is right there in our own backyard as the saying goes, or inside of us; all the time. We have learned many, many lessons in separation, and the Father loves us even more when we finally realise that the only way to find our true peace is through turning back to our beginning. We are loved more than the angels who have stayed by his side, when we finally turn back and reach for the arms of our Creator.

Freewill gives us the chance to learn. This planet, with its dense atmosphere, is one of the few with free-will in so great a degree. Our planet is so populated at this time by souls returning to learn the tremendous opportunities for growth which are being offered as Earth passes through its transition into the new Age.

At some stage in our lives, we often cease to find purpose any longer in the usual rush and bustle of our outwards lives, and start searching for real meaning to life. Why are we here? There must be more to life than just to exist, eat, procreate, work and die? There comes a time when we start to question the reasons behind our existence.

We are all made up of energy. That energy is from Source, or ultimate intelligence. There had to be a Creator to create that energy. Nothing comes from nothing. Energy is created from mind, from thought. There has to be the thought first before physical matter comes into existence. Spirit is that energy. It is spirit that creates physical matter. We are not a physical body with a spirit. We are spiritual beings, and we created our physical bodies exactly as they are; through, and by, our very thoughts. The physical body is only important in that it is our vehicle to carry us through this life, in order to fulfil the purpose we came to accomplish.

Death of the physical body does not stop us learning the lessons we came to learn. Life is an ongoing adventure; each time continuing on through the cycles in an ever-expanding spiral. If we could but realise that we create our own circumstances in order to learn and to grow.

Karma is being brought to the fore at this time faster than it ever has before. We are in changing times. We are being given an opportunity to live out the results of deeds we have done; or have neglected to do; in order to cleanse them forever from our souls. We can overcome our past karma by learning to love all that comes to us unconditionally. The changing times are happening so quickly, many are overwhelmed with the speed of the things happening to them. Everything that we have ever done is catching up with us, and all our thoughts and deeds will soon be revealed for all to see. The Bible says of these times "nothing can be hidden from their eyes".

This is the time now to wake up and realise our true potential. This is the time to wake up and know why we were born. We are immortal beings and the reason we were born into this existence is to learn to give and experience love. Nothing else has any reality. Nothing else can be taken with us when we pass from this mortal existence.

Chapter 2

RELEASING JUDGEMENT

ONE OF THE THINGS THAT are important for us to realise as we become more enlightened, is that we have to let go of things like judgement, criticism, hurt ego and separation. Knowing this, doesn't make it any easier. The greatest philosophers throughout the ages have emphasised releasing of judgement as the way to greater freedom, and it is still being brought up as an issue. This means of course, releasing the judgement we have of both ourselves and others which amounts to criticism in any shape or form. It does not mean lack of discrimination in seeing a danger when it approaches, or in ignoring our inner voice. It means just that: releasing judgement or criticism. Until we learn to do this, we cannot find true freedom or enlightenment.

I was going through a bad stage, judging and criticising my husband for various reasons, and I asked for Divine help in overcoming it. The answer I received was:

> *We have mentioned to you before that the only way to find unconditional love is through non-judgement and acceptance. This applies very much now in your husband's case. Observe, but do not judge him. He is indeed being a reflection for you. See in him what you lack in self. His life is one of service and giving. He is tired of not being appreciated. Send him your love, your understanding, and most of all, your acceptance of him, and acknowledgement*

of him as a perfect being in God's light. He is shining his light in his own way. He is serving well. He has great need to take time unto himself for rest periods. He feels afraid to do this. He bears his responsibility heavily, and feels that to let go of this responsibility would be to let others down. Help him to recognise the love within himself. Show him your appreciation of him for just being who he is. He needs your love and support now more than ever. Go within and seek his eternal self. He has much to face within himself. Be accepting and forgiving.

Releasing judgement is one of the hardest things we have to learn to do to reach a stage of enlightenment. If everybody on the planet could accept all that is, without judgement, our planet would become enlightened immediately into the beautiful star it was always meant to be. Unfortunately, we are brought up in societies that are constantly judging, compartmentalising, and criticising others for being different. Every time we label something as good/bad, black/white, tall/short, etc. we are judging it with preconceived ideas. If we can accept things without making too many judgements about it, we feel a warm glow inside, as we release the blockages which cause our emotions to come to a stop.

We are in a separate reality to our brother, neighbour, or co-worker, every single day. The only way to overcome this is to look at everyone we meet, everyone we speak to, and everyone we read about, as if we were looking at an aspect of ourselves. We should then acknowledge that aspect of ourselves, and accept it, rather than trying to hide it. It is surprising how hard it is to recognise what we see in others as part of ourselves, or as a mirror of ourselves. Often it is part of us that we refuse to acknowledge, hidden deep within us. It is through learning to love and accept every part of ourselves, even the so called 'shadow side' of us, that we learn to accept it in others.

I hadn't realised how often I judge other motorists on the road when they suddenly cut in front of me and I swear out loud to myself: "You silly idiot!" Wow that slipped out so easily. How easy it is to say: "Don't judge". We do it all the time! I had been watching my behaviour and realised I judged and criticised constantly. I was judging and criticising my husband for smoking and, because I have a very sensitive nose, I criticise him for smelling of cigarettes. Yet, although I don't smoke, there must be an aspect in me that I have not acknowledged, in order for me to judge him this way.

I know I don't take too kindly to criticism myself, so that in itself is a lesson for me. I had a terrible argument with my husband one night, over his critical approach to everything. I believe I was unjustly criticising him for reflecting back to me, my own attitude towards him so often. That has been a very valuable lesson for me.

If we listen to the news on television, we are bound to find ourselves inwardly judging or criticising. We may judge people for everything from being on drugs to murder. Until we can really understand those people, by putting ourselves in their place, or "walking a mile in another man's shoes", as the saying goes, we cannot really understand life from their perspective. Everything in life has a cause and effect. These people may be having family troubles, or physical or mental ailments, which are part of an inner soul karma which they have to work out. It is not up to us to judge them. We are responsible for everything we see and do. If we see them as "bad", then it is because they mirror a judgement we, ourselves, place on ourselves on a subconscious level.

I know of people who are very much against homosexuality. But if homosexuality had no relationship to the way we think, why should it affect us so? If we see things from a different perspective, we would not be tempted to judge others the way we do. We live very much in social mores and see life from that perspective. If homosexuality, for example, was accepted as normal in early Greek times, and our society tends to be less lenient towards it on the whole, then is it fair to sit in judgement of something merely because it is scorned in the more conservative social circles today? How can we judge from the point of view of society today? Isn't it fair to accept that each individual has a right to be just as he is, and be more open to another's way of being? Isn't that what unconditional love is all about?

Each individual is working towards his own karmic path in life, and it is up to each to find his own way, in his own good time. Is it fair of us to be judging others when their lifestyle has no relevance for us today? How do we know we haven't lived that kind of life another time? I once heard it said that we have all been everyone at one time or another throughout our existence. Think about that one! If each of us had been everybody else, aren't we judging ourselves when we judge another?

Those we often disapprove of are usually reflections of ourselves. It is usually something within our own natures which we are secretly condemning ourselves for, which causes us to judge others. It is amazing how many times we judge others. If we stopped to think about it, the very things we judge them for; or disapprove of; are *always* something in ourselves which we cannot accept, have buried, or refuse to acknowledge. If we had no conflict within ourselves, we would not even be aware of any conflict from their actions, because it would have no meaning for us. *We cannot judge something of which we have no understanding ourselves.* That is something many will deny, but how can you sit and judge child molesters if you have never had any angry feelings against children at some time or another? You will say this is very different. But is it? We do not know the reasons or understand the circumstances of that person's life. Is it our place to judge them? Surely the law of karma will work its own way out for them. How can we judge homosexuals if we have never had any sexual feelings towards another which we have not fully understood within ourselves? Of course we want to deny these things, because we want to feel good about ourselves, but does anger and hatred really make us feel good about ourselves?

I once heard it said that if we could read a whole newspaper from cover to cover, and watch the news on television, without making one single judgement, that is, accept what we read and hear without any judgement, we are well on our way towards enlightenment. Try it! It's not easy to do. Our whole lifestyle is made up of judgements and decisions, categorizing and labelling. We are constantly criticizing, even ourselves. Watch yourself during one day, and see how many times you find yourself judging others or yourselves. Do you look in the mirror in the morning and criticize your appearance? Do you reprimand yourself if you make a mistake, or are late for work, or realise you've said the wrong thing?

Judgement of oneself is our worst enemy. One day I was feeling terrible: tired and not well, and asked help from Divine Source. The answer came:

> *Your mind is tired. Your body is tired. Let yourself rest in the arms of love. Do not be afraid to let go. There is a cushion of love ready for you to rest your head upon. Allow self to melt into it. Do not fear for the future. It is all taken care of. All is happening as it is meant to happen. Simply allow. Do not try and force any situation—just go with the flow. Be open to receive answers as they come. When you are fraught with fear or worry you block answers and they cannot be felt by you. Be aware of all things happening to you and around you. Be open to these things without judgement.*
>
> *We are always here and will be here with you throughout eternity. Resist the urge to judge self. This will bring about great disappointments for you if you do not stop judging. Release it all to God every night and allow the spirit to renew each day with freshness and light. Do not worry about the past—it is gone. The future has not arrived. Take each moment of time as if it is the only one in existence. Your worries will be no more. Only the good survives physical death. All else is transmuted into the ethers and becomes richness for future growth. Be happy always.*

The past is gone. The future has not yet come. This is the moment of now. All our judgements are based on past experiences or future fears. We have to try and live in the now. If we can accept ourselves exactly as we are, by *loving ourselves totally*, we will find it easier not to judge. It must begin with us. To release judgement, we have to first learn to love and accept our circumstances, ourselves and others as they are.

When we flare up in anger at someone, and we judge them wrongly, we may be judging them for something totally in error. What we are actually doing then, is judging them from *our* perspective and not seeing life from *their* perspective. In a situation like this, we may be actually *mis*judging them. Not knowing the whole story, we may be placing ourselves in the dangerous situation of putting our judgements on them, and actually cause them harm.

Releasing judgement is one of the hardest, and yet one of the most important lessons in reaching enlightenment. Imagine if all of humankind ceased to judge his brother. If *no-one* placed any judgement on another; what a different world it would be.

True judgement is non-judgement. When we pass into spirit, *we* are the ones who judge ourselves. We are not judged by an outside God. Everything is inside of us. We become our own judge and jury, with the help of our guides and the loving beings around us, as we review our lives and make decisions on how to improve ourselves the next time around. Everything everyone does is judged by *them*, by their Higher Selves, or their God-Self when they are forced to face their true Selves on the next plane of existence.

Criticising ourselves is what we tend to do here on this earth life. We are more critical with ourselves, more often than not, than we are of others. We pick on others if they do not conform to our standards, but what we are actually doing, is saying: "You don't do things according to *my* standards. You hurt my ego. Therefore I am criticising you". Our ego is our barrier to releasing judgement. It is the ego which tends to rule us, instead of being our servant.

When we subconsciously judge ourselves, we are being self-critical, for not measuring up to the standards we expect of ourselves. It is our ego saying: "You are not worthy, or you are not doing it right". Try to listen instead, to your inner voice, or intuition. This voice is not a critical voice. It is a loving, guiding voice and bears no criticism. When you realise your true inner voice has so much love for you, you will learn to love yourself, and you will find it easier to love others. The inner voice is a gentle, guiding voice and will never lead you astray. It will put you on the God-ward path every time.

Our ego is our sense of separation from ourselves. It is the little part of us that tells us we are individual, separate, or different from others. It gives us our distinct personality. But it prevents us from feeling "oneness" with others. We are all of the same spirit. We are all interconnected. Without our physical bodies, and our egos, we are all one. When we are fighting within ourselves for our individuality, we are pushing others away, and judging them because they are "different" from us. We do not understand ourselves, so we do not understand others. They are merely being a reflection of us.

When we see the old man down the street totally intoxicated, we are seeing a reflection of our own fears of isolation being expressed through his need to drink. He has used drink as a way out of facing his fears. He will eventually have to face his true reality. We are seeing our own refusal to acknowledge or face our fears mirrored in him. We are denying our own feelings and not truly understanding ourselves.

The only way to begin releasing judgement; is to accept ourselves exactly as we are. Total, unconditional love and total acceptance of every part of us is the only way to release judgement. Through accepting ourselves in totality, we are allowing all things to just be as they are. Once we can do that, we will find everything else easier to accept. We can then begin to realise the pattern our lives are taking and we will be well on our way to living in unconditional love.

Chapter 3

THE IMPORTANCE OF LOVE

T RUE, UNCONDITIONAL LOVE IS LOVE that accepts without question. It is love that allows. It does not criticize or judge, but continually loves without expecting anything in return. Imagine being accepted and loved by others just for being who we are, without any expectation in return. How many of us have wanted to be loved for just who we are? love is the only thing we carry with us when we leave this plane of physical existence, because it is the creative energy of the universe.

Without love nothing could grow. Flowers spring up through love. Stars and planets are created from the love of the Creator. After all, there is an old song which says: "Love makes the world go round." Love is the substance of which all things are created. We are made in the likeness of God; the spirit of God; the spirit of Love which is God. You may wonder why I use a capital L for love. What I am referring to is the unconditional Love and not the love which has been associated with lust and very loosely termed love, the word love having been used for everything from love of food to love of football teams, popular movies etc.

Most of us feel unworthy of love a lot of the time. We expect it to come to us, without really loving ourselves enough to feel we deserve it. My divine guidance answered me when I felt I was being punished for something with the following:

15

My child it is your own lack of self love. You feel unworthy of the great love of the Creator and you reject the gifts your Creator is offering you. You have as much right to the love of the Creator as any other creature upon your planet, or any other. Trust in all that is happening. Know it is for good purpose. Nothing is for no reason. All things will be understood in the long term. The waiting and testing period is from whence your strength comes. This is indeed the time of greatest learning.

Find joy in each circumstance. Laugh and be happy despite your troubles. They will melt in the face of laughter. All things are healing. When you lift your vibrations to a heightened state through joy and laughter, you will no longer feel the pain. It will seem irrelevant. love the being that is you. It has served you well. Take courage, be strong, and be of good cheer. Your heart will be fulfilled and all things will come to you. Lift up your eyes to the light. love all beings and be happy. Our advice to you today is to love and be happy. We love you greatly.

True love is when we let all things pass through us without judgement, in total acceptance and allowance. It is through this that we learn to love ourselves unconditionally, and thus we learn to love all that is around us, all people and things that are within our light as we radiate it outwards to the world.

We often criticize and fault others because we feel unworthy ourselves that we try to fault others to make them feel unworthy too. Many of us are brought up with criticism; it makes us feel worth-*less*. We are children of God and as such *are worthy* of love. We have to realise our *worthiness* and we will come to realise our full potential and why we chose to incarnate when we did, and also why we chose our own particular circumstances. We will then begin to learn the lessons in life we came to learn.

One time when I was berating myself for my feelings against someone else, I received the following answer from my divine guidance:

You are a unique manifestation of God-essence. Learn to understand your own Divinity. Do not be angry at what you experienced. You needed to experience that. It was part of your lessons in this lifetime to understand parts of self. Others follow their own path. It need not be yours. It is not yours. Each soul essence will learn in its own way.

For you now is the lesson of love. Let it flow forth from you freely. You have much to give. The challenges you face are those you chose to face before entering into this incarnation—to learn and understand. Let the understanding flow through you. Do not block it with fears of what might happen. All is happening now. Do you know that each time you let go of your feelings of separation you are becoming light. Indeed you are coming closer to your God-essence. Is not that what you want dear child?

What is the most important thing to you? Is it to hold onto what you cannot control or to let go—to find the flow again and move into the All-that-is.

Be happy. Each challenge is further growth. Live it with joy and be graceful and loving to all. You have no idea of the impact this has on others or of the light you radiate and send upwards when you do this.

We congratulate you on having come thus far. You bear our light. We are ones of the spirit—you are our form. Be glad and be exceedingly joyful. The days are coming when you will be filled with the light of God. Do not doubt our presence. We are the higher beings of your soul essence. love all. Serve all. That is the way to Truth, Light and Glory.

These words left me somewhat overcome. I feel there is no doubt of the existence of divine beings, those who are ever-ready to help us and guide us towards our true light. It is through opening to this love that our answers come.

Sometimes we feel unloved because we feel let down in some way. We then play the role of "victim" and we sometimes, subconsciously, manipulate others into being our "rescuer", making them feel responsible for our plight. In doing this we are, in effect, taking their energy. We are *refusing to love ourselves enough to accept total responsibility for who we are.* There are times we may not like ourselves, but by accepting ourselves when we get angry, hurt, or demoralised in some way, we come to realise that this is the lesson we chose to learn: to *overcome* things.

So often we reach out to others with blame. Then we feel guilty. This is typical of what we do when we are defending ourselves against a possible attack from others. It blocks our natural flow of love. Every time I berate my children for coming home late, I feel bad about it. I know within myself that it is not their fault. It is my own fears within me that I am reflecting back to them. Hence, I feel guilty afterwards. Having lost one child through a road accident, it is not easy when the others are late home. I believe it is like a defence mechanism against what we fear will happen

It is important not to blame ourselves when we do not meet our own expectations. Sometimes we blame others when things don't go as we wanted them to, but more often than not we are harder on ourselves than anyone else. It is important not to berate ourselves when we do something that we are disappointed with ourselves for, or for not doing something we wished we had done. All we can do is make the best of every circumstance, and accept what is. If we do not meet our own expectations, we can accept the fact that we are not perfect—*yet*—and know that the lesson will surely come again, perhaps in some other form of learning. We are never deprived of the chance to learn. We have to realise that we wouldn't be here if we were absolutely perfect. This earth plane is the schoolroom of life. It is where we come to learn our most important lessons. Treat every experience as a *learning experience*. Our greatest lessons in life are learnt through our "mistakes".

Through challenges in our lives we grow. It seems a hard lesson to find oneself in a situation where one loses a loved one, a job, or goes through a painful divorce. Yet there *are* lessons in life from all this. If we can approach each obstacle as something to be overcome; by taking a positive attitude; life becomes more enriched and fulfilled.

Our ego is our barrier to finding happiness. We have to overcome the constant little voices of "should I do this?" or "should I do that?"

or "what will happen if I do this?" or "would it be better to do that?" We have to be firm in our actions. Procrastination is our greatest downfall, because we never take the risks in life. It also locks down our system of energy. Through taking risks, we learn. There are no right or wrong decisions. Everything in life is a challenge. If we sit and do nothing in life, we go nowhere. We do not grow.

I believe we take on human form to learn, to experience love, to understand the responsibility of living in this world. We cannot face responsibility if we sit doing nothing. We have to actually *do* something in order to learn. It is by our "wrong" actions that we learn what not to do next time. That is how we learn. A child is told, time and time again, not to touch a hot iron, but he or she will inevitably be drawn to the hot iron until they learn it is plain hot by touching it themselves. Teenagers are told not to speed because it causes accidents, but how many teenagers still speed? They have to learn this often painful lesson when an accident occurs and results in injury or the further shock of loss of life. It is like a process of elimination. We learn through finding out what not to do. The challenge is there for us to face. Try it and discover what is right for you.

Giving is so much more rewarding than getting. Many feel they are in this life to get money, wealth, or possessions. Yet with all these things we find that they become our goal and we become increasingly dissatisfied the more we get. On the other hand, if we start out by giving, we grow richer the more we give, because we are giving from ourselves. It seems to satisfy a soul need and we find the rewards enriching our inner life. No matter how little we have in the way of material possessions, we always have something to give, even if it is just a smile. Things given away from a totally selfless perspective; enrich us far more than anything we could ever receive. Everything actually comes from our Source, or God, and what we are in effect doing, is giving back, or returning to Source, what we have received. The only thing we can take with us on leaving this life; is the love we have experienced.

A multi-millionaire in Sydney donated four million dollars to the Salvation Army. He has also donated to other worthy causes.

When asked about it, he said it was only on loan to him anyway. That is the way a truly evolved soul responds. They understand that to "have" is only temporary. They realise that by giving freely, they are far richer. There is nothing wrong with having. It is the 'owning'that gets us into trouble. It becomes our possession and eventually, it can get such a hold on us, that instead of us having something, it will possess us!

Nothing is ours forever; except love. Our children will one day leave us. Our home will one day fall down and decay. Our bodies will someday disintegrate into dust or ashes. There is nothing of a physical nature that is permanent. Only the love we give and the love we receive are enduring. It is the spiritual essence that evades everything, that should be our goal. By giving freely of ourselves, we enrich that essence and thereby grow to become richer than our wildest dreams. Our basic essence is that love.

When love comes from the heart, it is like the opening of the heart chakra. You feel your chakra expanding, almost like an ache. The love you feel is there for everyone. I was once with a group that did an experiment. We went to a busy shopping centre and focused love on people. We would sit in a coffee lounge or on a seat somewhere and send out love to people around us, beginning with a particular person. We would imagine what life would be like for that person and visualise their circumstances, feel great empathy with them, and send them love. Once we had made the initial contact (and the person would most likely turn and look at us so we had to then turn away), we could focus on anyone and the same feeling would occur. We then found that we felt this open love for everything. We even felt love for the chairs and the street poles, the plants and the footpath we walked on. It just radiated outwards like an ever-expanding aura of light.

Unconditional love is like that. It asks nothing in return. It just allows all things to *be*. It accepts all and offers itself to everything that comes within its focus.

When we have learned to do this, we can also send absent healing in the form of love to others, by visualising them, and seeing them surrounded with light and love. There have been situations where I have done this, even with someone I have had difficulty loving in person. I have found that animosity evaporates, and you find you can accept that person as they are, if nothing else. When I next had contact with that person, the situation was calmer, and it was easier to break down the barriers.

Human love is always asking for conditions. "I'll love you if you do such and such for me". "I'll only be loved when I do this or that". It creates a fear of not being good enough, of unworthiness, in us. We may say, "He doesn't love me, so I don't love him either!" That is not unconditional love. I have found myself saying this sometimes. It makes us realise that we do not have enough self respect for ourselves, and we believe the love has to come from outside of us. But real love has to begin within us. We cannot give away what we don't have. We cannot love others if we don't first love ourselves.

The late Avatar, Sathya Sai Baba from India, was said to have spread unconditional love. Many people had been gently scolded by him in a very loving way, and they have felt his total all-encompassing love fill them at the same time. We are all capable of this cosmic love, yet many find it too difficult. It is only through *experiencing* this kind of love that we can come to understand its unlimited potential. Many believed Sai Baba to be God. He was indeed a most holy man and believed to be the Avatar of the age. He told us we are all God but we do not know it yet, whereas he has reached full awareness of his own God-potential. His miracles were many, and there are many books on him. He tells us he comes to us from within.

I once felt the words:

> I am ever with you. Does it matter if I travel to you or you travel to me? We are together. I am <u>within</u> you. I am the one who writes these words. I am in you always. The flesh body is such a temporary abode. Half of your physical life is spent out of your flesh body. When you sleep, you leave your body to rest, and travel inwards to the greatest journeys you will ever take. Lift up your consciousness. Lift up your light. Let it shine.

So much of your life is spent in sadness and doubt. Be conscious in each moment. Be aware of my presence within you. I Am the Light which shines through you. I am the inner knowing. Listen to your inner voice and you will never need to be afraid again. I am he who is with you now. Allow yourself to experience me and feel my presence. I am the one and only, the All-that-is, and I am in everything. You ask where I am. I am in the pen that writes on this page, I am in the presence of every object in this room. I am the very breath you breathe. My love is ever present in you. Let this love flow outwards. You have much to give. Sing, be joyful, and live to the fullest extent you can. Never be afraid for I am ever present—within you and around you at all times—forever.

Oh, the power of love! This powerful thought, coming through my pen, uplifted me greatly. It revealed to me the power of love that is in and around *everything*! Love can heal anything. Love can create anything. Love can *do* anything. There are no limits to what true, unconditional love can do.

Love begins at home. Like all things it has to begin within ourselves. We have to truly love ourselves first and believe we are worthy of it. In this society we have had it drummed into us from our early days, that it was wrong to love ourselves. This is the greatest untruth of all times. Sure, the ego is always prompting us to love our personality self, but loving of our true Selves is a totally different thing. Our ego has tricked us into thinking we are selfish to love ourselves. Without acceding ourselves, and knowing we are what we are because we chose to be, we would become unbalanced. That is precisely why society has so much unbalance and disease today.

How do we lift ourselves up from despair and depression? The weight of the world is on our shoulders and we feel so heavily burdened that it is almost impossible at times to rise out of this heaviness. We are even too down to think of asking for help. The days of depression are long and hard. We often get sick. These days can be alleviated through restful sleep, or by simply going quietly within, and looking for the answers within ourselves.

How many times are we depressed? It is a state of actually not loving ourselves enough. When we are down or depressed or unhappy, it is actually that we do not value ourselves enough. We are not valuing ourselves as much as our Creator does. We are not allowing ourselves just to *be!*

Too many times we live by our past reactions. The memory of past hurts effect the way we react to a situation. Our fears rise to the surface, and we find ourselves flaring up in defence. We create this defence as a way of protecting ourselves from being hurt. We feel vulnerable and are afraid of being hurt again. This is how our attitude to our fellowman can cause separation and hatred, which in turn has more world—devastating effects. In the world view, for example, wars are caused by this very attitude. Fear predominates. Fear of loss, fear of a country being invaded or hurt by another nation. The media bombards the masses with the glory of war which conditions men's minds to believe it is the "only way to go". This is a great fallacy. When will humankind learn that the only way to live in peace is through unconditional love and acceptance of one another. War is *not* the answer. Only through loving our fellowman, which begins with *self*-love, can we attain true peace.

Love is so much stronger than hate. It can truly transform the world. Thoughts of love can actually reach people. Everybody in their inner heart is searching for love. Many do not know it, but it is the only true reality, and those who seem to be vengeful, hurt, angry or jealous, are actually calling out for love. They are sending out signals saying: "I want to be loved". They have all the love they need within themselves but they do not yet know it. Love *must* come from within first, before it can be radiated outwards to others. It is *not wrong to love oneself.* In fact it is the most important thing for us to do. Jesus said to "love others *as* you love yourself." He never said not to love ourselves. It is not vain to love your Self; your true inner self; because unless you do; you cannot possibly love anything outside of yourself. *Seek within*, not outside of yourself for the richness of love.

We are not talking about the ego here. The ego is that part of us that is separate from everyone else. We are talking about the part of ourselves that is in oneness with the Great Spirit, God, or Creator; that part of ourselves that is actually joined with the spirit part of everyone. Through understanding and loving this part of ourselves, we learn to love others, because they are also joined to this divine part of themselves, which is part of the all.

If we look at the other person as being a divine part of the whole, we are looking at the divine part within ourselves, and we are seeing them as ourselves. We are all equal—no worse, no better than anybody else. We are all creations of the One Creator. No matter what stage of growth we are all on, the spirit is the same within everybody. Some are just more aware of it than others. We are all on a path of growth: growth towards the divine light which is our true selves.

When we love, no matter whether it is a little bird, a pet animal, or a child, that love is never lost. It is an energy that radiates out to the universe. It spreads, firstly to the object of our love, then into the ether. It makes up the stuff that permeates the planet, and indeed the whole universe. It is the energy that creates. It causes life to go on. When we leave our physical bodies and join with the ether, the love we felt while in our physical bodies; stays around us. We re-unite with it as it were, and it feeds our souls. How important love is!

If you could imagine a life lived with no love, you would be looking at a dead soul. A soul that feeds on hate, envy, greed, or selfishness is a soul that does not know how to communicate to the universe. It is a soul starved of the very substance that feeds life. It would be deprived of its very essence.

Our true essence is love. It is an opening to the universal energy. We are connected to this energy, and when we feel love, we are opening to this energy. When we lack love, we are closing off this energy, or separating ourselves from its source. When we feel separated through despair, hate, envy, jealousy, greed, or selfishness, we are locking ourselves away from the very substance of life.

My divine guidance answered me when I was asking how I could release my jealousy which I didn't understand with the following:

> *In order for it to be released it has to be accepted and acknowledged. Only by embracing it and bringing it up into the light will it be released. It is your refusal to face it that is your worst enemy. You are afraid of the unknown. You have been hurt in a previous life and it has left you badly scarred. Forgive yourself, and forgive others. This feeling of fear and jealousy will not mend, until you learn to forgive self and others and bring it into the light.*

But how can I do this? I asked.

> *It is by allowing self to feel the full passion of the feeling. It is by riding the waves as it were, and not trying to block or prevent this feeling. You will find it is not nearly as bad as you fear once you have faced it square on. Dread not dear child. Only your own fears are holding you back from great enlightenment.*

Forgiveness stands out prominently as the opening for the beginning of self love. In every situation, forgiveness is the first thing we have to do if we want to find our pathway towards releasing our negative feelings and finding the true love within. My late daughter, in her diary wrote, "*Love others as <u>yourself</u>*". Even she realised that to love others, you have to first love yourself. Being aware of the importance of love is the first step towards creating a more fulfilling life for ourselves and others. Once we begin to realise how important it is to love, we can take the next step of asking for help when we are in trouble or need. Help is always available, and prayers are always answered.

Chapter 4

~

WE *DO* HAVE HELP

W E *DO* HAVE HELP. MANY times I have asked for help and the answer has come. I do this sometimes in a form of prayer, sometimes by picking up paper and pen and writing a question that is burning in my heart for an answer. If I relax my mind enough, the answer will flow through my head and I write the words without really thinking about them. I feel myself lifted out of myself somehow, as the answers flow through me. It is only afterwards, when the transition has stopped, that I re-read what has been written and am quite astounded at the profundity of what has come from my divine guidance. Sometimes it is in the plural and sometimes in the singular. I know there are guides and angels helping me. When the answers come in the singular, I feel it is more an answer from my Higher Self, or God-Source.

We all have divine help from the spiritual realm if we wish to tap into this valuable source. These beautiful divine beings are ever willing to help us if we only ask. They cannot do anything to help if we do not ask, even if we only ask in our minds. We have to recognize that they are there, and ask for their help. This is the importance of faith and prayer, and meditation. It is vitally important at this time on planet Earth, to use the divine energies available to us for healing of ourselves, others, and the Earth herself. These great spiritual beings are just waiting for us to ask them. They can help us help ourselves. These are our spiritual

Guides, the Masters and angels who are also part of the One-God, and those who have travelled the same road as we are on. When we ask for help, they are thereby empowered to give us a helping hand when we find ourselves in a situation which is less than desirable. They are there through the good times and the bad—as we judge them to be. There is no judgement as such in the spiritual realm, as all is accepted for what it is.

The energies *do not judge* us. They supply what we ask for. If we put out feelings of unworthiness; that is what we will find ourselves becoming: unworthy. If we put out feelings of fear, we are validating it and giving it a greater reality. These things come back to us many times multiplied. If, however, we put out feelings of joy, that is what comes back to us, in greater quantity than we have dreamed possible. *We are our own creators.* What we put out we get back. We create our own future, *by our thoughts!* If we have feelings of hatred and fear, we actually put this into the ether surrounding the planet, and it is there for the collective consciousness to pick up. We *darken* our planet with these thoughts.

It is most important at this time to *lighten up*, both for ourselves and for the sake of the planet Earth. The planet has been carrying our burdens for so long, while we have pillaged and raped her, and she is beginning to feel the birth pains of a new beginning emerging. We must raise our thoughts to lift ourselves up to the higher vibrations as the earth is raised also to a higher vibration in the coming of this New Age.

The divine guidance spoke to me about my chance to overcome my negativity:

> *Today is your chance to overcome your negativity. There are many questions coming into your life at this time. Each division is a greater chance for growth. With help from your guardians you can overcome this negative force. Ask for our help and we will be there. Let others face their own challenges—you can help them more by allowing them the right to face their own selves—their own battles.*

Remember to ask us in your mind to help, and we will be there. Go forward with strength. We encourage you to go forward. Looking back will achieve nothing. Love self and all else will come to you. Your strength comes from a higher source. Allow it to flow. When you block this flow with your fears, you actually stop your growth, as you prevent us from helping you further. Relax. Try and meditate tonight and we will help you to go into yourself. Let go of grudges. These are a hindrance to the soul. Allow yourself to live each moment to the full. Live each moment in joy. There is much to celebrate in just being alive. Treat this situation as a gift and allow yourself to enjoy it. It is of great benefit. Love what you do and do what you love. Take the best from each moment. Live in love.

We *can* do something to lift these dark clouds around the planet. We can transmute them with love. Love is a real force. It is the *strongest force in the universe* and nothing was created without love. We can look at a situation where we have been hurt, and say: "Well, I was hurt or angry in that situation. I accept that. I am free from that feeling now. I love that part of myself that was hurt. I embrace the child in me that was hurt. I am love."

It is important to ask for help by prayer, or requests to the higher forces. Every thought we have is prayer in some form. Much help is needed on earth at the moment and there are many willing in the spirit realm to help. But they cannot help us unless we *ask*. By asking for help, we empower them to help us, and they in turn empower us. There are many beings that will come to our aid, depending on what we ask for. We must make sure, however, we ask only to the highest being, as there are low entities that are also willing to help create mischief. We should always go to the top: to God Himself, in our prayers. Because there is no judgement in the higher realms, whatever we ask for will come to us. That is why it is important to ensure we really want what we ask for, because we will get it! Know that it will come, and it will. Do not have doubts of your prayers or requests being answered. They will be answered if we do not invalidate them by doubts.

We should not ask for things to boost our ego. The higher realms will not oblige if what we ask for is not in alignment with our highest good, but is for selfish purposes. We are more than likely to get a nasty surprise if we are not in alignment with our spiritual purpose when we ask.

Once I asked my divine guidance for help for a friend who was having some personal problems. The answers came:

> Through looking deep within, the answers will be found. She has much guidance which needs to be acknowledged. Too often you ones on planet earth see the illusion for the reality. The truth is in everything. Truth lies buried within the heart. Love is the only true reality. Fear creates judgement. Without judgement there would be no judging of right and wrong, for all would be allowed to just be. Know that God does not judge. All life is experience alone, and learning to love all things because they are, not because they do. This is the true aim of life and the path to peace. All is not as it seems. Your friend has created for herself many judgements which must be released to find peace . . . She must try and let go of the concept of what others think, and shower her love without restraint. All will work out for the better. Lessons are being learned. Remember, love is truly the only antidote to every ill. Let it shine forth in its true glory.
>
> None is ever alone. There is much help. Your friend is quite psychic and must use discretion. Let love be her guide. We hope this has helped.

Time and again, divine guidance points out the importance of love as being the only answer to our many problems and our many obstacles. The above is no exception. Here, also, is expressed the need to use discretion. It is only with love in our hearts, that we can bring answers from our divine guidance, and not from a lower source.

Many times I have asked for help in understanding my true purpose in life; the reason I came into this existence. I am getting stronger and stronger feelings that it is to show others the truths

I have come to realise. Many books have just come to me as I scanned the shelves of book shops, and I *knew* they were right. It is an awareness that one seems to have. You seem to just *know* when something is meant to be for you. I have actually had a book literally fall off the book shelf once, when I was looking at another one. These things *do* happen, and I believe it is our spirit friends helping us to help ourselves to grow. There is no limit to what we can do. Often we place limits and conditions on ourselves, and this prevents us growing spiritually as much as if we "go with the flow" and take everything that comes to us as a step in our growth.

We should not limit the expectations of our prayers or requests. Sometimes we ask for something so specific, and outline how we want it, instead of letting the universe bring it to us in whatever form it comes. We have to be open to recognise the answers when they come. This is important, as, if we make too many demands we are limiting the potential of the universe, are not leaving ourselves open to look for the answers in whatever form they come. A friend of mine wanted to sell her house desperately. She was determined to get a particular sum of money for it, and when the chance came for selling at the exact time she wanted to sell, the money was not up to her expectations, so she refused to sell. She may well have been receiving an answer from the universe for the immediate sale of her house, but by placing limits on the *exact* amount of money as well, she was not allowing the universe its full potential.

It is necessary to go within for the answers when we are confused or unsure about things which happen to us. We should really think about things before we rush into them, and meditate on whether something is right at a particular time. We are told Jesus meditated about whether the time was right for him go to Jerusalem at a particular time, hence his delay in entering that city when he knew what awaited him. By going within, or meditating, we are able to decide when the time is right for particular things in our lives.

So many times I have felt critical of a co-worker for trying to control everything in his path. Little did I realise that what I was seeing was a reflection of how I, myself, am at home. I had been trying to control things at home, and was frustrated at it all being totally disorganised when my husband was painting the house, and everything was out of my control. Hence I felt miserable and helpless.

If we can just let go of this control, "let go and let God", as the saying goes, how much lighter our lives would become. We are creatures of materialism. It is not easy to not have things around us as we wish them to be. It is not easy to have no control of our surroundings, especially when it is our haven after a hard day at work. Sometimes the only way to overcome misery and depression; is to *ask* for help from a Higher Source; God, angels, the universe; or whoever you feel is your highest power in life.

When you ask for help with a heart full of sincerity, your prayer *will* be answered. *"Prayers are always answered"*, we are told. The universe always answers prayers. It is sometimes our expectations which are not in alignment with the answers when they come, and we must realise not to expect things to be a certain way, because the universe may answer in a way we least expect. We *must be open to whatever answer comes*. But help does come. It may be through a dream, or an unexpected person's reply, or through something in the mail, or even through a thought which just pops into your head. But *always*, true, sincere prayers are answered.

One response I received when I felt I was not helping as much as I should have, came with very direct answers. A little of the response has been deleted as it was a very personal question which was being answered.

> *There are many you can help. Simply being willing to listen is the first step in helping them. You have a great ability to give to them by showing them your compassion and being ever-ready to offer a response when it is asked.*
>
> *Every step you take in the direction of learning is a greater step in your own growth. Your own learning is being given ever greater opportunities through the contact you have with others . . . We will provide the answers to your requests. It is all being attended to. Your son will find his job. Have no fear that he won't. Your family are*

all being looked after. All it takes on your part is love and acceptance, and more love. Never be afraid to give your love. You have much to give and many depend on it, both on your side and on this side. Your wishes will be granted. Have trust in the universe and in life. Remember that the great I am is always with you. Love much always.

My son did indeed find a job as promised by my Guidance, and I have no doubt that all my other questions will also be answered. All we have to do is ask.

Chapter 5

FREE WILL AND THE EGO

W E WERE BORN TO LIVE in joy. We were not born to suffer. We sometimes choose experiences such as suffering as an experience on a soul level, but it is not the intention of the Creator that we should suffer. This earth is the schoolroom of life, but we can live and learn in joy.

Our lives follow cyclic changes and mood frames, brought on by our birth times and the influence of the positioning of the stars and planets at certain periods in our lives. Astrology is a very real science, unlike the daily astrology the newspapers and magazines generalise in giving out. The actual position of the planets at the time of our birth, *do* have an influence on our lives. They help to shape our character. There are many millions of people, for example, born under the sign of Gemini or Pieces, but each one is different because there are a multitude of other influences affecting them. A genuine astrologer can help you discover certain influences that affect you, but they need not be taken as gospel. We can utilise these influences to our advantage, and be guided by them, but we need not let them override our free will choice in our lives. There is an abundance of joy in the universe. We have to look for the joy. We have to look for the happiness and potential that exists around us in our everyday lives.

There are times in our lives when we may feel lonely and bereft. We feel no-one loves us and life is not worth living. We

35

feel "out of sorts" and cannot come to grips with anything. How do we lift ourselves out of this mood? The best way is by trusting in the universe. Know that it is good and that we choose these situations for our potential to grow. We grow more in the 'bad, sad times', than we do in the happier times. If we lived on a cloud all the time, there would be no challenge; no growth. It is through finding the best in these bad times that we face the challenge, and can thus transmute all our past karma. By bringing the more negative aspects of ourselves into the light, accepting them, and finding some degree of joy in the situation, we actually cause a chemical change within ourselves. By accepting our mood as part of ourselves and saying: "Well, I love this part of myself. I chose this in order to grow. I bring it to the light."

Once my guidance told me:

> *Dear one, you are never alone. All your life there have been presences around you, helping you and surrounding you with their love and attention. They never interfered, but sometimes they ached to. Their arms where near you, just waiting to reach out and embrace you, but you did not realise this and you kept them at a distance. All that you had to do was ask. It is as simple as that.*
>
> *Loneliness is only felt when you separate yourself from your Self when you let yourself part by pushing away that which is always meant to be a part of you. Every part of your many aspects is connected—much like electricity is always connected and only has to be activated for many things to begin to happen. When you turn on a switch which has many plugs attached to it, you can turn on a multitude of attachments at the same time, and light up appliances all over your place at the same time. And you know that all electricity is connected. It runs through all homes in all cities in all countries at the same time. Therefore it is always there. It is only by turning off switches that you cut yourself from this source of electricity (unless there is a power blackout—laughing—which of course is like others taking this source from you but in fact this is not what happens) . . .*

So you see, when you turn off your "switches" you push away the connection that has always been there for you. In all your years, how many times have you called on us? It has been infrequently compared to the many times we have waited and watched and wanted to comfort you. You are never alone. In your quiet times of solitude that is when we come closest to you. We whisper in your ear, we light up the light in your head, and we hold your hand and comfort you. We send you love from our hearts to yours, and we envelop you in this love like a cocoon enfolding the chrysalis. All we do is love you. And we are always there.

When you separated from the source, you never really separated. There was always an invisible thread of light, which held you to us. We are spirit beings of light and we are connected to All-That-Is by other beams of invisible light. We hold you in those beams. Even in your deepest, darkest hour you will find us there. When you are desolate, deprived and sad, you will find us waiting. When you are isolated and imprisoned, you will find us beside you. When you are ostracised by society, and thrown out of home, you will find us holding out our arms to comfort you. The road you travel seems lonely, but it is only in your perception. There are many hidden prizes waiting for you along the way, which have not yet revealed themselves. Be observant as you walk your path, and you will be surprised and delighted at what will appear before you. We are waiting there, holding these presents for you, and holding you in our presence. Know, always, that you are loved.

Imagine every part of your being filled with light. We have the free will to take the negative aspect of ourselves and simply allow it, without letting it affect others. Treat it as part of yourself, which it is. Don't try to fight it but allow it to be. By loving it and accepting it, you are acknowledging it and can transform your negative shadow side thereby becoming a lighter, more loving being. The lesson you chose will then be being learnt, and you will have a deeper feeling of satisfaction than you have ever felt, because you have transmuted the negative by accepting it, into a positive, joy-filled experience!

There is no limit to what you can do. Only our ego tells us there are things we cannot do; things we have to be afraid of; things that we have to categorize and separate. All things are from the Divine, and by acknowledging all things, and allowing them to just be, we overcome the forces of the negative/positive poles which surround us in a world of duality. This is how we bring about the changes to our planet. By not judging, but instead, accepting all things as they are, being joyful about every situation, particularly the bad times, we actually can overcome our karma and save ourselves from continuous re-births. This is the way back to the God-head or Source.

We are all actors in the stage of life. Our God-Self is the director and producer. We are merely the actors; learning through the experience, and eventually taking that experience back to our Source. All things are experienced through us, as we are part of the Great Spirit. We have free will and ego, but if we submit to our little self, or ego, it will eventually become our master, and we become slaves to the ego. To find true freedom, we have to find the higher source of our being, our God-Self or Higher Self, and let this Divine part of ourselves guide us through life.

In the chapter on Releasing Judgement, I talk about the ego being the cause of much of our need to judge, because it separates us from others. I call the ego the Great Separator. It is not, in itself, a bad thing. It is very useful for us in maintaining our individual identity. But it must serve the Greater Self instead of being the master. We have free will. This free will is our freedom to choose between giving reign to our ego, or little self; and allowing our Greater Self to guide our lives in alignment with the Source or Universe.

If we look at life from a truly spiritual perspective, we tend to see everything has a purpose, and become less attached to the "things" which feed our ego. It is our attachment to these things that cause us to have desires which pull us closer to the physical, instead of the spiritual bodies we really are. Our ego is afraid of losing itself to the oneness. It continually dissects and slices everything into sections to be labelled and separated into categories. It fills us with temporary pleasure and reminds us of the pleasure or pain we experienced last time. Both pleasure and pain are illusions of the mind. Socrates debated this point to some of the greatest minds in Greek history. Deepak Chopra, in his book *The Way of the Wizard*, states:

"Self image separates; labelling things. It uses an image of a past experience to judge something. It will say *I like this because it gave me pleasure before, therefore it will give me pleasure again.* Pleasure is temporary . . ."

By allowing ourselves free will, we allow the "little ego" to have its way. Our Greater Self knows that this is not the way. Within us are both the little ego and the Greater Self. We have to allow both these parts of ourselves to exist side by side in peace. The only way we can do this, is to let the Greater Self lead the smaller self, or ego. In other words, let our ego become the servant instead of the master.

When our free will is in alignment with the universe, our ego rejoices. It does not mind being put in its place. It is like a child who needs restraining. It is happy to know it is loved, and yet is still allowed to be. It is happy to serve.

We can know what our Greater Self is telling us, by going quietly within and listening to the inner voice. We can then follow the guidance we receive. Some call this guidance a conscience. This inner voice really does talk to us and help guide us through our lives if we are still and listen!

If we can find our balance between our free will, and the Divine voice within, we are well on the way to doing the will of our Creator. Ultimately, we will all find our way back to wanting to do the Divine will. Until that time, we still follow our own free will and it will repeatedly lead us astray, until we learn to recognise what we all are really seeking, and that is to do the will of God.

Just as our little ego is willing to be put in its place if it is loved and accepted for what it is, so too, can we serve our fellowman with respect and acceptance. One of the best ways to reach enlightenment; is through love and service to our fellowman. No matter how humble our job, it is doing whatever we are given in life to do, *with love*, which will lead us faster towards the path of enlightenment.

Often a near death experience (NDE) can result in our seeing things in a new light. It seems to result in the ego standing aside, once we see a glimpse into the "real" world that is awaiting us. These experiences seem to have one thing in common: they all have life changing results. One such story is of a five year old child, who was admitted to hospital for a minor surgical procedure. The boy was given too much ether which caused a brief respiratory failure and possible cardiac arrest. With that, he experienced something which changed his life: he felt strong love emitting from a being of light followed by a review of his short life. He wrote many years later:

"I re-experienced everything that had happened in my life and watched it as a spectator with the being. Most of what I saw was about me and my brother, of whom I was very jealous. My attention was focused on our exchange of emotions, my jealousy, my feelings of triumph when I hit him, his surprise when I hit him for no reason, his anger and resentment, and later his triumph when he got back at me."

He also experienced the few loving moments he had with his brother:

"When I did something loving to him, I experienced my love, my brother's surprise, as well as his love and happiness. I experienced his feelings as clearly as my own, making this a fantastic lesson on the consequences of my own actions. It was the love from the being of light that gave me the strength to see my life exactly as it was, without making it better or worse."

It appears that when we look at our lives objectively, we experience, not only our own feelings, but the feelings we cause others at the same time. This, it appears, is what it is like when we pass from this life to the next. So if we are jealous towards another, we are deemed to experience their feelings towards us at the same time when we re—live this experience. Our perceived view of separation brought about by the ego's individuality, is no longer there once we re-join others in the spiritual realms.

Chapter 6

LISTENING TO THE INNER VOICE—
THE GOD WITHIN

G OD SPEAKS TO US FROM *within*. That is the only way we hear Him. It is through our imagination that we hear Him. Joan of Arc was visited in prison by a friend who said: "Joan, if you will only say it is your imagination they will let you go." Joan replied: "It *is* my imagination." The friend sighed with relief. Then Joan said: "How else could I hear God speaking?"

Sometimes I hear voices in my head which make a lot of sense. They calm me down, and when I listen to them, they answer all the flighty questions the other part of my mind comes up with. Like when I ask "where am I going? What am I doing with my life?" the voices have answered me with:

> *You are following the path which is before you in order to learn the lessons which you chose to learn. You chose to learn these lessons, and until you overcome them you will not grow in the way toward your Greater Self. What you are doing with your life is learning. That is life's purpose: to learn and to love. love is the greatest thing we can do with our lives. We are here to grow in love and wisdom. When you can love even that which you thought you hated or were afraid of, you have taken a huge step*

41

forward in your growth. You can teach this love by giving to other people what you have learned. We are showing you in dreams what you can do. What you cannot do in your daily life, you are able to connect with in dreams. You can actually meet these people on the astral plane and give them loving advice which helps both undo any bad karma which you, or they, have collected during this or other lifetimes.

I feel confident and calm with these voices. I feel it is a collective of wisdom. It does not seem to judge me, but will advise me if I ask for advice on a particular problem in my life.

We must not doubt the voice that comes from our imagination, even when it doesn't sound logical to our left-brain way of thinking. It is more often than not the voice of our God within. It is through our imagination that we hear this voice. I believe I have heard the voice of my daughter through my imagination. After my husband painted the house, I was sitting on a chair in the family room and I imagined her as she was, and the statement: "I like what Dad's done Mum. Its ace!" came to me very clearly. I wondered at the time if it was just my imagination. But that is exactly how my daughter would have said it.

Your imagination can be your best friend. We create all our own reality and our view of the world by the way we see or imagine things.

How can we know which is the ego talking to us and which is a Higher Voice? By the quality of what is said. I believe it is through the gift of imagination that we have all our answers, and when we stop the chatter-box mind from prattling on, we can go quietly enough within to hear the voice that is our inspiration, our guide, our conscience, and our God within.

I have been told by divine guidance that I did not need to do anything to achieve a higher state. They expressed time and again, that simply by letting go and relaxing, I could reach this state.

Yes we are close. Your efforts to reach a higher state are not necessary. We are here all the time. Do not try so

*hard—just let go. Through relaxing you go into a higher
state of consciousness, a higher part of yourself. We, your
guides, your guidance and your higher vibrations, never
leave you. To tap into us, all you have to do; is simply
let go of your lower mind. Let it relax, and in so doing it
ceases to control you any longer and we are able to enter
your conscious mind.*

*Indeed you are closer to heightened vibrations than
you thought. You do not have to travel away from your
home, or away from your environment, to find your wish
of heightened vibration. We are here, as close as your
breath, at any time you choose to relax and let go. There
are many others you can help. Just be yourself. All the
strength, all the knowledge, and all the energy is within
you. We send our love, and the light which is you grows
stronger every time we communicate through you. Simply
show love to all. You connect with us in this way . . .*

There are many who claim they do not believe in God. Yet
there is a very real force out there, and within us, which causes all
things to grow. Without this force all things would disintegrate,
but because there is this force, all things are transformed or
transmuted into something else. Ice becomes water; then turns into
steam when heated to a certain temperature. All things become
something else when they change form, either a gas, or ether.
There is nothing that does not become some other form. Even
our bodies become the dust of the earth when they disintegrate,
which in turn enriches the soil and thereby helps things to grow.
Nothing can come from nothing. God simply *is.*

Everything first exists as a thought in the Mind of God.
Everything is God. There is nothing that exists that is not God-
Source. How can any deny their own existence? Every person is
living proof that God exists. How else could they, themselves be?
We are all living examples of the creation of our own God Source.
Our own thoughts created us. We are part of All-That-Is. Each
being is a microcosm within the macrocosm, the miniaturization
of the whole universe. We all have the potential to become

everything. There is no limit to what man can do when he takes on the responsibility of his own God-Source.

Meditation helps us listen to the voice within. It is through meditation that we discover our true selves and begin to delve into our purpose in this lifetime. There are so many types of meditation. Some use visualization, some try to clear the mind, and others drift into another state of consciousness. I find soft music helpful. It depends on your particular type of requirement and what is right for you. It can vary from time to time. Sometimes a quiet place, or a walk in the forest among nature, can be what is needed. Do whatever brings you into alignment with the Source, nature or oneness that is you.

Meditation helps us to find our true purpose in life. It is only through going within that we find out who we truly are. Many times in this day and age we are caught up, rushing from one thing to another, and we miss the whole point of being here on this earth. We get caught up in survival mode, and forget that we are eternal beings who are here at this time to learn the lessons our souls chose to learn.

Earth is like a schoolroom. Each of us learns by the elimination of our more negative natures. That is, a person may learn not to kill, but he has not yet learnt the lessons of anger or hatred, so he chooses to come back to learn to love instead of hate. Another may have learnt not to kill or hate, but has come back to learn not to steal or deprive another. He may have chosen to have things taken from him, so that he can learn what it is like to be stolen from. These are very basic examples. Life is very complicated and complex and no two cases are ever alike. We create what we need to learn, in basic form, before we enter this physical existence and because of our free will choices, there are many different ways we can learn our lessons. If we do not learn one way, another way will present itself. And if we don't learn this particular lifetime, there is another lifetime, and another, in which to learn.

Through meditation we can feel this inner voice and we become aware of these lessons at a deeper level.

Our guides are *real*. They are here to guide us on our journey through life. Once I doubted their existence and I really thought for a moment that it was just imagination. Yet what is imagination? The answer that came assured me:

> *The answers are not from you my child. They are from us, your guides. We were given the role of guiding you in your lifetime. Some of us are from the higher realms; some are closer to the earth plane. There are many of us. You came into this incarnation with a purpose. We are here to guide you in that purpose. You have an opportunity to assist many. Let this begin without further delay. Do not let your fears override you. They hinder you. There is nothing to fear. All is unfolding as it was meant to. Take opportunity to go within to the rich resources of your soul. Let us guide you. We do influence your dreams also. All is coming out into the light of knowledge at this time. There is nothing of such darkness that it cannot be healed and forgiven.*
>
> *Let things unfold naturally. Take time for self to listen. Loftiness is in the eye of the beholder. Let your feelings pour forth for they are the natural way of life. Do not be afraid to express these feelings for their eventual exposure is imminent. Love all who enter your path with a full heart. Be as natural as you can be. Others will relate far easier when they see your human side. Let it all be accepted and acknowledged. Your light radiates when you are experiencing your true self. Let it always be so.*

The above came as answers to my unasked questions. I had been afraid of expressing myself and my natural shyness was difficult to overcome. Many of the situations in my life at the time were facing minor difficulties. Yet, always the answers come. It is through these answers that I am learning.

We are told there are many, many lessons for us to learn before we reach the end of our soul's journey. We have all lived many times in physical form. We have, at some time, been everybody. Many of the traits and characteristics we carry with us today, are from previous lifetimes, and the more prominent attributes are from the lives that are affecting us this lifetime so that we may learn from them. We do not remember these experiences, although the soul alone remembers.

Many of our phobias come from past lifetimes. Things like fears of spiders or mice, or fear of heights may likely be from an experience where we actually died from spider bites or from falling off a cliff. There are many different experiences with may be attributed to some lifetime where the lesson has not yet been learnt. If we remembered everything from every lifetime, we would be driven crazy, and would not learn the lesson we came to learn, because we would not then have the experience of knowing the other side of the play. We are all actors upon the stage of life. We are caught up in our life experience in order to learn and experience those lessons which our soul has chosen in order to improve and to grow more towards perfection and towards our oneness with Source.

I believe dreams answer a lot of our questions and show us how our life pattern is forming. The biggest challenge is in knowing how to interpret our dreams. There are many books out on dreams and dream interpretation, but only we can know the real meanings behind our dreams, because it is us that is the dreamer. Sometimes someone else can help, because they can pick up something which we, ourselves, have not thought of. But it is us that provide the vital clue to our dream, and it is only through being totally honest with ourselves that we can learn to interpret and understand what our dreams are telling us. I was told that our divine guidance also influences our dreams.

Many believe dreams are just the subconscious mind, or the replaying of something we watched on television. This can be the case, but there has to be something in the program we watched, or in our subconscious mind, that triggers some deeper feeling that needs attention. By recording our dreams, or noticing the patterns over a period of time, we learn to understand what we are being shown about our life pattern at that time.

We have our dream children. It has been said that each time we make love; we are creating a spirit child. If this is true, there must be many little spirit forms in the ether surrounding this planet made with thought forms that we created. Many times I have dreamed of little children, or babies, and I have felt great love for them. I question if this is part of my inner self I am seeing. Is this the child within that needs nourishment?

Every part of our dreams has something to teach us. If we can turn and face the things we fear most, they become transformed into a more benevolent force. They are all lessons in teaching us to love ourselves more. My daughter once dreamed of a monster who was trying to get her and she resisted it again and again. Then she finally turned to face it, and it became a blob which put its arms around her and said, "I only wanted to love you." The dream ended in its transformation. She seemed to have an insight into how to transform her dreams. We can transform our dreams by facing our fears and learning from them. If we can love our most frightening aspects, we can transform them.

If our dreams are trying to tell us something, we should take note of what happens when we call for help in a dream. If we call out to God or someone in whose authority we trust, to help us in a dream, we are never left wanting. Always someone comes to our rescue and we are able to disengage from the situation and find a better solution.

It is the same in life. We do have help we can call on. Our answers, however, more often than not, come from within. There is as much life in the world we cannot see with our physical eyes, if not more, than what we can see.

The Divine Guidance has told me repeatedly to live in joy. Sometimes we have to quiet the intellect in order to listen to the quiet joy within our soul. This message was from a single Divine source:

> *Believe that which is in your heart. Be joyful. Let not things others say or write disturb you. The truth is within. Outside influences can only activate that which is already*

within you. Love from the depths of your whole being. Share what you feel with love. Do not be hesitant in showing this love. All that you have is Mine alone. We are one. The deep love in your heart is the love of God within. There is no separation. Be one with others. Allow yourself to feel for them but do not let their intellect influence your "knowings". There is much true knowledge within everyone, yet many times the intellect or mind, takes over and will not allow the true feelings to come through. You must guard against this happening to you. Be open enough to allow your love to flow forth freely. This love is deep and strong. Nothing that exists can override the love that is within your heart. All things will come to you as you allow this love to flow outwards. You are all children of love. Let not your heart be troubled. Know that I am within you at all times. Simply allow the love to flow. Be at peace.

Chapter 7

~

FREEING ATTACHMENT

TRYING TO FREE OURSELVES FROM attachment to the things and feelings on this third dimensional plane is not easy, but is an important step in reaching enlightenment. Holding onto the things we feel we want and need, is a natural reaction. The spiritual path teaches us that it is necessary to detach from these things if we are to find true freedom and peace. It becomes one of the hardest lessons in life, particularly in our western world of so many material possessions.

My divine guidance gave me the following advice:

> *Material possessions are like a ship passing in the night.*
> *Do not get so immersed that you cannot escape from the*
> *material world into your quiet times. These quiet times*
> *are necessary for your soul's upliftment and renewal. The*
> *quiet times provide the soul with the nourishment which*
> *is necessary for its growth. Food fills the stomach, but*
> *true satisfaction comes from harmony within the soul.*
> *Through coming into quietness you will find peace in*
> *your heart, and soul food. Do not neglect this side of*
> *your life—this is how growth occurs. Take as much joy*
> *as possible from every situation in your life—taking and*
> *giving, loving and forgiving—that is the way happiness*
> *and true peace within the heart will abide. Through love*
> *peace will come.*

Love is not a material possession to be bought and sold. It is a mystical vibration which exists in all dimensions. It is your essence. It is the essence of all life. If you lost your connection to this love, you would find life literally without meaning. You would die inwardly without love. Allow yourself to love, and to forgive. Too many are holding onto negative thoughts of hate or revenge even against themselves. To find this love within your soul, all thoughts have to be released—forgiven and accepted. This is the path of unconditional love.

We have spoken of this before, but it is so important in your lives it must be emphasized. Love all, serve all, and do not hold any grudges. Live and forgive in every situation. Find your peace within. We leave you with blessings of the most high.

As Divine Guidance tells us, we are holding onto negative thoughts when we hold grudges; do not forgive; or refuse to accept anything. Our thoughts and habits are also things we need to become detached from. By looking at each day as a new day, we can let go of thoughts of the past and see each moment as it is right now.

True detachment is totally accepting everything we see, feel and touch without judgement. When we see someone dying, it is natural to want to do something to prevent the suffering, but if nothing can be done, we can learn to accept death as an ongoing process of life and let them pass gracefully. When we see people hungry, we can offer them food, but this may fail to satisfy their soul need, and we have to learn to accept that they chose that experience for their own learning. This does not mean we should refuse to help. It means we become detached from the emotional pull, and do what we can to help, with unconditional love. Sometimes those in pain are choosing it from a soul level to learn their lessons. We have to understand we are *not* the body. We are spiritual beings.

Those things we see outside of ourselves are reflections of what is going on inside of us. That is, if we see someone who is angry, and we react to it, it may be well to look within ourselves, as we may have some hidden anger in us. If we feel someone is critical of us, it is because we are reacting to it, and we are holding some criticism inside of us.

Many of us have blockages. We do not realise what is between us and finding our True Selves, or enlightenment. We want to rush forward and reach our goal, without going through the important stages of learning the lessons along the way. Such traits as stubbornness, or clinging to things like our anger or our guilt, can hold us back from our path. Sometimes our lessons are revealed through dreams.

I had a dream which showed me I was still holding onto my stubbornness. I know I do have a stubborn streak, but I never realised before that it was actually holding me back from advancing spiritually. When we are on the path towards enlightenment, or finding our True Selves, the ego begins fighting for its last vestiges of individuality, because it is afraid of losing itself into the All-That-Is. This is not what happens when we merge into that great Oneness. We never lose our individuality. We become part of the All-That-Is but we retain our individuality.

Our ego easily accepts the fact that roses bloom by themselves and embryos form naturally, but it can't accept this fact about money, houses, relationships and other things it gets attached to. Ego gets attached to certain energy forms such as money, houses, relationships, and it cannot relinquish these "attachments" because it is afraid of losing the desire it holds over these wants.

If we tend to judge desire we are judging its source which is us. If we fear desire, this means we fear ourselves. There is nothing wrong with desire itself. Desires are what we are meant to have in order to grow. Without desires we would stagnate! We would be like a frozen icicle in space. We would have nothing to get us motivated in order to experience life. Desires get thrown away as new ones come along. They are meant to be used as stepping stones which we utilize along life's path, in order to reach our goal in life. The problem is not with the desire itself, but with what happens when our desires are blocked or frustrated. It is then that the struggle and judgement begin.

Detachment is not the same as indifference. When you see suffering, go and relieve it, but don't come away with the suffering stuck to you.

If you don't accept the earth has spirit, you may think that because she doesn't complain she is indifferent. There is a vast difference between detachment and indifference. Detachment can become indifference. It is in the name of indifference we are destroying the earth. If you kick a rock, it's you who hurts. The earth does not cry out when we kick her. She is secure in her spirit. We can learn this detachment by accepting ourselves and thereby becoming secure in that acceptance.

It is only when we can walk away from a situation which confronts us, without reacting, that we are on the way to detachment. By doing this, we can find true freedom. We become freed from the things which pull us towards our reactions to others. It is better to act rather than react in any given situation, because we are then masters of our own lives and not pulled into the back and forth motion of the ego's little game of separation.

Mother's Day was an important lesson for me, in that first year especially, in freeing myself of attachment. It is very hard to let go of someone you love. It is even harder when they are no longer in physical form. This is a day when Mothers are remembered, and those who have lost children, feel most bereft of all. We have to let go of material attachment. It is one very prominent lesson, and not an easy one. We have to tell ourselves that wherever our children are, in whatever sphere or plane or country they are in, they still love us and we them. Love is the only important thing, and it is *permanent*. When you love someone or something, it is never lost.

More often than not, we are attached to our emotions. We are attached to our anger, our hatred, our needs, our criticisms, and our judgements. Because we are in a physical body, it is very hard to stand back and look at ourselves objectively. But to release ourselves from attachment to these emotions or needs, it is necessary to watch our reactions to everything that occurs in our daily lives, particularly in relation to others. As we react, we release an emotion. It may be anger, frustration or even jealousy. The feeling may not easily be controlled. This is where it can help to stand outside of ourselves and watch our reaction without actually getting involved in the reaction. Let the reaction occur, and just watch it. If you can look at yourself objectively, you can almost laugh at your reaction when you see it is the light of the greater Self. Once we realise that everything that happens to us is caused by our own reactions alone, then there is nothing that is really out of our own control.

Having been brought up in the mores of society, we often struggle to do what we feel is right. We may be afraid to do or not do something for fear of losing the approval of others. We may feel we do not want to give of ourselves to others, and yet feel we have to. If we follow our inner voice, and our hearts are open, and we give for the right reasons, that is, give from the heart, through love, and not because we feel we have to, we do not get involved in the terrible pang of separation that otherwise would isolate us from our true feelings.

What is important in letting go of attachment, which is easier said than done in today's world with all its many material possessions, is to live in the moment, accept what we have but then to release it and let it go! We can become as little children and live in the moment, not worrying about the future, or fretting about the past, but living totally in the now! It is a little like letting go the edge of a cliff instead of hanging on, when we find ourselves falling, and learning to trust in the power of the universe. Trusting in God is like that. We have to learn to have total trust and faith in the goodness of the Universal Energy, called God.

It is not easy to free ourselves from attachment. I have found myself clinging to things like problems and feelings, even more than material attachments. Being a stubborn person, it is harder to let go of the emotions which attach themselves to me. One way to help us let go, is to realise that every bit of unwanted emotion we cling to, we take with us into spirit when we pass from this form of existence. If we really want freedom, we have to let go. If we really want to leave our problems behind when we pass on, we have to begin doing this now. The fruit of our labours begins now and each and every new day is an opportunity to begin afresh; living each moment as if it really counts. If you could just imagine each moment of now being your last, how would you live it? What we do, and think now, determines our next plane of consciousness.

Material success does not necessarily denote soul growth. There are many unscrupulous beings who have "made it to the top" in the material world by stepping on others on their way up, or by eliminating others who were in their way. Real success in life comes from the extent of soul growth; how much we have learned through our failures.

Sometimes the time comes to let go of certain stages in our lives. Some of us do not like change. We are frightened by what might happen, and we cling to what we are familiar with. Once I put this to my divine guidance and their answer was as follows:

> New avenues are opening up to you. You know the saying "when one door closes another opens". You have glorious prospects ahead. Your deepest desires are about to be met. Have no fear. Fear will bind you. Fear will constrict you. Fear will block all avenues of channel, all avenues of light, and prevent, for a time at least, the new options coming into fruition for you. Love is always constant. Love always abounds. Be aware always that life goes on!

Our fears toward "letting go" are fruitless. By taking a chance, and living in the truth of the moment, we are released by the truth, and our bindings are freed.

There are many earthbound spirits who have clung to objects and deeds of their earthly life, and have not been able to ascend into the higher planes of consciousness because of this.

It is the actions and thoughts of today, that create the future for us. In this way, we create our future ourselves, each and every moment of every single day. We are co-creators with God and through our thoughts we create all that we are. We created our very essence by the thoughts we generated. We created our trials, our successes and our failures by our thoughts and actions both now and in past times. We do not realise our own power. We have power beyond our wildest imagination. It is so very important to be in alignment with our true spiritual purpose, to be in alignment with God's will we have to reclaim our power back again and take full responsibility for everything we do.

Chapter 8

LETTING GO OF FEAR

T HERE COMES A TIME IN everyone's life when we have to face our shadow side or negative side. I woke up one morning with a very strong feeling of seeing myself as jealous. It was not a pleasant feeling and I realised that it is based on a feeling of fear; fear of loss. It is something that has been very much below the surface most of the time. But nevertheless it is something that is probably colouring much of my daily life on a subconscious level.

When I asked for Divine Guidance on my problem the answer came:

> *Jealousy is fear of not being good enough. It is an aspect of fear—an aspect of lack of self love. It is one of the most harmful diseases upon your planet today and the most damaging.*
>
> *It can be transmuted by total self love—self acceptance and knowing your God within. It must be faced—brought out into the open and understood for the harmful disease that it is. Only then can it find release and be transmuted into oneness with all. There is no need or necessity for jealousy my child. It is your own illusion of fear which brings it about. Face your fears head on. Bring them into the light. Name them for what they are and they will have a hold on you no longer. Be willing to release your jealousy and your fear of insecurity into the light. You will*

57

> discover, when you have done this, the most wonderful
> feeling of security, knowing and trust, that you have ever
> felt overwhelm you.
>
> Know that you are immortal and nothing can harm
> you. You are your God within. You are all that is, and if
> you can truly love every aspect of yourself—jealousy will
> not have a place in your life. Be open with your feelings.
> Love all, serve all. But most of all, love self in every way.
>
> We leave you with the promise that this feeling you
> have will be released. Trust in the universe. Trust the
> Creator and know his love for all.

We have to face these feelings, acknowledge them, and accept
them for what they are: feelings of fear, insecurity and lack of
light. When we bring them into focus, we actually bring them
into the light and they then cease to hurt or destroy us any longer.
I started to analyse why I felt this jealousy and I realised it was
based on a fear of loss. This was later confirmed by my guidance. It
is probably the most predominant fear we humans have. It is quite
an understandable feeling when we think of ourselves as being
mortal beings with limited life or limited existence. But what we
have then failed to realise is that we are not the body.

We are far more than our physical body as we now think of it.
We are immortal. We live time and again, and each lesson is a very
valuable lesson in facing ourselves and who we actually are. We
are not the body. The body is our vehicle to carry us through this
life experience. We can make it as pleasant or unpleasant as we
choose, but in the end, we come to realise our own immortality,
and the fact that we do go on. By releasing these feelings of fear,
jealousy, hatred and hurt, we are coming into contact with our
own immortality. We are letting the light of knowledge shine forth
through our person. We are becoming light.

Fears are part of our illusion of time. If we could see life like
the man in the plane, looking down at the little boat in the river,
instead just looking at life from the limited perspective of the little
man in the boat, not seeing where he was going or where he'd
come from, we would be able to let go of some of our fears of things

to come. All things have their time. Nothing is permanent. Only the Creator Himself is unchangeable. Have no fear. This is a new beginning for you. Be of good cheer. Let your love flow outwards to everyone.

There is only now. All that has ever been, or ever will be, is within us right now. We are the sum total of all we have ever been, or ever will be. We are All-That-Is. We have total control over our lives by our thoughts. No-one has any power over us except ourselves. The only way anyone else can penetrate our thoughts, our lives, or affect our reactions, is if we let them. We do have power over our own thoughts and thereby can control, and are totally responsible for, all our actions and everything that happens to us!

I asked divine guidance to help me. I said I was afraid, especially of the big things.

> *Your fears are not cemented in reality. There is nothing about change to fear. Nothing is ever lost. Be of good cheer. Only the illusion is altering. All things will be better for you. Take heart. Change is necessary for growth! Nothing can exist without change in some form . . . Know my love is ever with you. I am your constant companion. Remain calm in each step of your life. Let serenity be your guide. Only you control your thoughts and emotions. Let them be in peace.*
>
> *The world is waiting to understand its own peace. Each individual has to find his peace within his or her own heart. Love grows from within. Understand that all things perceived by you are as they appear from within. To change thoughts of hurt, fear or sadness, first alter them in your mind's eye to make them joy, peace and comfort. Transmute them all with love of self. All things are changeable except the love that is deep within your essence. That love is the very being of you. Humankind, wake up to the love that is your very essence . . .*

We have often blamed others. It is the way we have been brought up. It is so hard to break conditioning that has been drummed into us from little babies. We have to undo all our past thinking and take on new ways of thinking. The only limits to our universe, to what we can do, are in our minds. Our own fear holds us back! Think about that one. If we could release fear totally, there would be nothing to limit us doing anything. We could change the world by loving every obstacle in our lives, instead of fearing it! It is really as simple as that. Just imagine, if we could never get sick, never have an accident, always be supplied of an abundance of whatever we wanted, and lived forever in our physical bodies—if that is what you wanted. There is no limit, except in your own mind. Only you create that limit.

This book would not be complete without some mention of what my guides said about accepting our shadow side of ourselves. They told me that a chapter on this topic was important because this is where humanity is heading. They said:

> This chapter will balance out that which you have already spoken of regarding acceptance and non-judgement and allowing. Words can be clumsy things. Sometimes just going into the feeling is better. Go into the quiet within and relax. The words that come through will then be our words. These words can be distorted by the conscious mind if it intrudes too much, as the words are flowing through. Do not despair that this will happen. Follow our guidance and we will assist you to write what is important for humanity to understand at this point in time.
>
> The future is a probable future. It is not written yet. We see it from the perspective of the whole, as time in the sense you view it does not exist for us. All things can be altered by the changing consciousness of man. We are here to see that this change occurs with the least possible upheaval to humanity. Those who have not raised their consciousness at the time of the coming changes; will either have a more dramatic experience which will alter their consciousness instantly, or they will exit their bodies and find themselves in another plane when this change occurs upon your planet.

That the change will occur is a surety. It has been decreed by the Spiritual Hierarchy and this will occur. Humanity has gone as far towards the negative pole as he can and has thrown the planet out of balance. His eventual return towards spiritual enlightenment is imminent. This may take many years in your terms—but it will happen.

This planet which you call Earth is a planet where the polarities were meant to exist in balance. It is this balance which will bring it greater light than even the most "positive" planet in the universe, because light and dark will be integrated and all things will be accepted. Once you realise that all things are allowed, they will cease to have the hold over you that they have had in the past. All is from the Creator. He expresses Himself in many forms. The Creator is expressing himself on planet Earth as both spiritual and material. These two are to be integrated into a wholeness which is one. Many are assisting the Earth in this wonderful transition. We look at your future and we rejoice.

We come into knowing of ourselves, and loving ourselves, when we accept our shadow side. There are things about ourselves which we may not like, but by acknowledging them and saying: "It's okay to be angry, or hurt or jealous. I'll allow this feeling and not repress it." By integrating our negative feelings and not denying them we allow them to just be. This is how we bring our wholeness into the light.

It is by this acknowledgement of our shadow sides that we can find the way to living a balanced state. The way to do this is by observing our thoughts, or reactions, when they come up. If we find ourselves getting annoyed at someone, for example, step back and observe our reaction and say to ourselves: "Why do I get annoyed by this person?"

More often than not, it will be because we have a part inside of ourselves which they mirror, which we have repressed and refused to acknowledge. If we are honest with ourselves, this feeling will be the root cause of our annoyance.

Acceptance of this shadow side of ourselves; is what brings about our transformation. Without darkness there would be no light. For us to recognise day, there has to be night. Both are necessary to find the balance which is all. Both negative and positive, feminine and masculine, nourishment and creation are part of the All-That-Is. Once we can integrate this shadow side of ourselves, we can emerge fully into the light of Truth.

Light would not be light, without dark to compare it with. In order or recognise light there has to be dark. God made both the opposite polarities like negative and positive in us, as in the negative and positive currents which run through electrical circuits. Without both we would not have electricity. We have to have night and day, summer and winter. If it was always summer we wouldn't appreciate it without experiencing the winter too. They can both be beautiful seasons. We can learn to find our balance in life by accepting both sides of ourselves.

Pain and Fear

I feel pain is often a part of our shadow side which needs to be acknowledged. Sometimes I suffer migraine headaches. I wonder if it is because I, myself, want to suffer. I know I don't on a conscious level; in fact I am afraid of getting a headache, because they have been so bad at times. This is where fear holds me back. I sometimes think it is my Higher Self telling me that there is something amiss, something I haven't done or should be doing. In some way I am out of alignment with my spirit or true purpose. To overcome these headaches, I have to go deep within myself and ask what it is that I am trying to avoid, or that I am out of alignment with. When I face this, the headaches will cease to be.

A little verse I remember from childhood came to me once when I was in pain:

Pain built a fence I was quick to hate. I clawed at the bars. They held me fast. But when I learned to be patient at last, God took my fence and made it a gate.

I asked God if He was really there to help me with my pain. I felt an instant response:

"My child, your pain is my gift to you." I realised then that pain, if we accept and acknowledge it without resistance, becomes our friend. It can be an ally to bring us closer to our inner self because it tells us more about who we really are. It shows us the path we can take to alleviate it, by seeing it as a lesson. It can be a valuable lesson sometimes; in patience and acceptance. Once we have learned this, the grace of God offers us a gate through which we can walk away from our pain. Truly our pain is a gift from God. The lessons we learn from our pain can become our most valuable teachers in our lives.

My guidance told me:

This body is such a small part of your being—yet it affects the whole. All of your multidimensional selves are affected by each thing you do, each thing you think. Remember the effect you have on others. How much more do you think this effect has on all your other selves. Be kind, compassionate and loving. You now know what it is like to feel discomfort and pain. Feel for others. They too suffer but they do not understand the reasons.

You have a greater insight into the reasons for your pain and discomfort. Understand that others are experiencing their own pain for the reasons chosen by their Higher Selves, for their own growth. They have not yet understood the capacity within them for greatness, or experienced themselves as multidimensional beings. They still feel they are only beings of the five senses. Be compassionate with them. Your learning is to become your greatest teachings. Others will look to you for understanding. You have the ability to give it.

Allow self to feel pain. Only by so doing will you be allowing it and understanding of its true purpose. If you try to ignore the pain, it will come again in another way, until you understand that it is to be allowed, embraced and accepted. It can only then be transformed into the light. Love all, serve all—even the pain within your body . . .

So often we are plagued by fears. If we think about it, these fears all arise from our perception of ourselves as the body. Sometimes these fears may be from what we feel we have done wrong, that is, a feeling of guilt, or from an experience triggering soul memories which are buried deep within us. Sometimes these feelings are so deep we do not even know why we feel afraid.

I have an irrational fear of deep water, and try as I might, I cannot analyse it to find out the cause. I believe it may be a soul memory causing this fear, from a past life experience. I may have lost my life in a previous time through drowning in deep water. Some experience must have caused this fear. The only way to overcome these fears, is for me to go deep within the feeling; visualising myself diving—and diving is another thing I just cannot do this lifetime—deep into the water, and know, know beyond a shadow of a doubt, that I cannot die. If I can know within myself that there is no need for this seemingly irrational fear, I can overcome this fear and transmute it into acceptance.

Worry is fear. It does no good to us or anyone else. It is a waste of energy that could be used for our betterment. I am constantly being told that our fears are illusions and the changing times are guiding us into greater light.

> *Take every moment as a gift from the Creator. Time is a gift from God. Each moment is now. Do not let past or future worry you. Each second you breathe is a new second, a new chance, to live as you were meant to live. Be cheerful. Be joyful. There is nothing whatsoever that can happen which can harm you. You are eternal. You live in eternal Light. Let that Light guide you through each moment. Your fears are your illusions. The only reality is the essence of you—which is total love. Follow your guiding light. If you remain centred in this light, there is naught that can ever harm you. If you become less centred or stray, it will only delay your eventual arrival in the oneness of All-That-Is.*
>
> *Live your life in joy—in harmony with all life—for that is the surest and quickest path to your own enlightenment. Enlightenment is the lightening of you. You become what*

you truly are. You wake up. That is what enlightenment means. Live in joy, for each step of the way is a chance to learn; another learning experience; another chance to polish up a point of the star which is you.

Be of good cheer. The world is coming into greater times. Many lights are being polished. You are becoming brighter in each millisecond than you were before. Be aware of your light, for in so being, you are able to awaken another's light—simply by being around them. You do not have to say anything—for words can be misleading. Simply be who you are and walk in your own glorious light.

There are so many fears we carry around with us, like a heavy sack of potatoes on our backs. We can shed these fears by following the advice of the Guidance. It is hard to dispose of our burden, because society has taught us that it is supposed to be that way. We have been conditioned from early childhood to be afraid; if we step out of line we will not be accepted. If we don't follow the mores of society, we will be rejected, an outcast. If we don't measure up, we will be a failure in society. How much these stigmas have patterned our lives. It makes us afraid of stepping out of line. Our whole conditioning has become part of our lives. The only way we can break this conditioning is to realise the effect it has had on us and change our pattern of thinking!

Nothing in life is stagnant. Change is a constant. Go into your fears. Feel the depth of them and analyse why you feel threatened. Is it because in times past you have had this happen? Know that there is no mal-intent in this instant. All things are happening for your own evolution . . . Take each day one step at a time . . . Do not hold back the flow but let it come freely. Were it not for constant change, nothing would evolve. Your goal of reaching the godhead is ever closer. Relax into the moment and simply allow all to be. Be not afraid. Just be aware of your constant stream of thoughts—and let them go. Come into the quiet within . . . Be at peace.

Fear need not be carried around like a burden on our backs. Because change is ongoing every moment of our lives, we can release our fear by allowing the changes to occur.

We overcome fear with love. These are the two polarities we face in life. If we have a choice which leads to some feeling which has a fear based emotion, then it is not the one we should follow. But if a decision leads us to feeling good, to a feeling of love and unity, then we are opening out into love. This is how we can make choices or decisions if we want to release fear in our lives. Love and fear; these are the two basic emotions from which every other feeling comes. Recognise the feeling for what it is; the first step. From there we make the decision that holds no fear for us. This, then, is the way home. This decision towards a love based society; is the way we reach our path to enlightenment.

Chapter 9

KNOWING SOURCE

W E ARE PART OF THE Great Divine. We are not separate from God, or Source. We are, and always were, a Divine aspect of All-That-Is. We have our lower natures, to be sure, but our spiritual aspect is the God within that is our Higher Selves. When we come into contact with this spiritual Source, the All-That-Is, the Creator or God, whatever you feel comfortable with, we meld with, and become part of our true source. All is God. There is nothing that is not of the Divine Source. That is where man has mistakenly separated different aspects of himself into duality. It is through understanding this aspect of ourselves that we become whole. It is balance and wholeness that we ultimately seek to become one with God.

I was told:

> Recognise your source as being from Divine origin. When you do this with self, you will realise that all others have their deepest feelings nestled in Divine source. When compassion for all, and understanding of all, is achieved upon this plane, unconditional love will be for all creatures, and peace shall truly reign upon your planet.
>
> When love is without duty, but purely from the heart, it is well towards becoming unconditional. Serving through love is Divine. Let your deepest feelings be your guide. Feel with your whole being. Do not block feelings.

Let them exist and be. Acknowledge them. All feelings are part of the whole. All have their roots in Divine source. Allow the feelings which are deepest to emerge into the light and they will be transformed by the love of God.

Every creature seeks love. That is the essence of all life. When total unconditional love is achieved, all things upon your planet will be healed. Give with your whole heart. There is naught you cannot achieve when you give with love. Love is a force stronger than any others. Compassion and love go hand in hand. Let understanding be your guide. Allow the light to enter all phases of your being and let it shine for all . . .

Over and over I am told that unconditional love is the answer to humanity's every ill. To find unconditional love for others we have to first find it within ourselves. To love ourselves is to love God. To truly know ourselves is to know God. Just being and recognising ourselves as part of the Great Divine is a step towards this enlightenment.

Our bodies often affect our everyday lives. They seem to be in control of us rather than us controlling them. Women have monthly cyclic changes which affect their moods, attitudes, and colour their lives generally. Also they are closer to the earth, as earth also undergoes cyclic changes. Their bodies are carriages for other life forms, and as such are influenced by more than just their minds. They are influenced by the life forms they carry when new life is within them; and they are influenced by the monthly patterns that change their bodies; which are affected by changes which take place as their bodies start to take on mid-life changes. Our minds are powerful, but they can have total control over these cyclic changes. Women are far closer to Mother Nature because they are constantly changing. They are more attuned with the Father-Mother-God and their thoughts and patterns of thinking reflect this. Men tend to be more brain-orientated because they are closer to a pattern of thinking rather than feeling.

It is important to sort out our differences and to love another, while we are still here in physical form. Our life experience is to learn to love. Each time we hate or criticise another, we are closing off our God-essence and locking down our chakra centres. We are blocking the natural flow of life!

Sometimes I feel like there are two persons in me; a strong, wise part of me, and an immature child. I asked how I could integrate these and feel more balanced:

> *By coming into the knowing, know that we are here to help you. You are not alone. You are a multifaceted being. You are not a single personality. Go within your depths and explore your feelings. Be open to the fact that there is more to you. Do not lock self into a single facet. Be aware that there are many dimensions at any time you feel low or depressed. Once the depths are investigated, they will no longer frighten you. They are just other facets of self that need to be accepted. Go within and accept them by loving and acknowledging them. Where do you think the word acknowledgement comes from? Knowledge of course; knowing becomes enlightening.*

We came to earth in spirit form to learn to love. This planet is a very dense planet and the lessons are harder here because of the duality we face. We learn faster here than anywhere else in the cosmos, because the lessons are harder. Earth itself is in a process of transition, or change. We are fast approaching a time when all our past, present, and future, will become one. It is important to recognise this, because everything we have ever felt, done or thought, will come again to be challenged. We will be tested, and to pass the test, the only way is to love everything and everybody unconditionally! It is the only way to win grace and free ourselves of the burdens which we now carry.

The earth is changing. It is a living entity and must be respected as part of creation. It, also, is evolving into a higher dimension. Humanity must raise his consciousness together with the earth, or be left out in the cold for another millennium.

We have been told by the higher sources that prayer is particularly important at this time. It helps keep our connection to our God Source. It has to be sincere and dedicated from our hearts. It is of no value to us or anyone else if it is not earnest and sincere. It is the message from the heart that radiates out to others and to the world. Self forgiveness is important. We are most relentless of all with ourselves. We may not realise how often we are seeing ourselves in others when we criticize or judge them.

By earnestly asking for divine help in overcoming our problems, we are creating a vortex of possibility for these events to be changed. We are thereby opening ourselves to change, and shifting our thinking pattern to allow the transition of change through our thoughts. By releasing one thought which we no longer wish to hold onto, we are creating a space or vortex for another thought to take its place. It is like a cup of water. If the cup is already full, there is no more room; therefore we have to empty out the contents in order to receive the divine nectar of love, forgiveness, and light. If we have raised our consciousness through prayer, we are allowing a higher thought to penetrate our minds and thereby change our perception, allowing for greater light to come into our lives.

Those who claim to predict the future are seeing probabilities only. The future has not been written. Probabilities are always changing as circumstances change, and man's free will is altered. Always there is a chance to overcome our future obstacles. In so far as the *knowings*, or feelings of just knowing, are concerned, there is certainly a Higher Authority controlling the greater picture, but within our life we have free will choice through which we can change, at any time, the future for ourselves. I do believe we, ourselves, have control of our own future by our perception of it. We are the ones with the free will to choose. We are the ones who make the final decision in any circumstance. We are the ones whose future this is.

Those who see "probabilities" for our future, are reading into our aura, and often they see the most likely scenario from what we have already done in the past in any given situation. Sometimes they may be picking up a "future" that comes to them from the astral dimension in which time is not like ours. We create the situation we find ourselves in. Therefore we have the choice to raise our vibrations and extricate ourselves from a situation if we so choose.

We are never left on this planet at any time without divine help. We only need to ask, and help will be given. When we are born, there is at least one guardian Spirit who remains with us throughout our entire lives, and many others who assist us during our sojourn on this plane as we pass through the different avenues of life.

When we pass from this life into the next, we are fully exposed to ourselves. All our thoughts, words and deeds, lay before us in a conglomeration of visions. We see ourselves as others have seen us, we see ourselves as we think we are, and we see ourselves as we truly are. We are faced with everything we have done, and left undone, in this lifetime. The regrets and remorse are upon us in full force. It is only through love that some light may shine upon us. We are our own judges. No-one else judges us, but we are guided by our own Higher Source and the love of the Almighty Himself.

Through the love we have shared on this earth plane we are taught to see ourselves for what we really are. It is through love that we break down the barriers of remorse and guilt. There are higher beings that come to us and assist us in this transition. Anyone we have hurt, whether knowingly or unknowingly, is seen by us. We then review our mistakes, and have a chance to redeem ourselves. But this can take many years in our terms of time. It is far easier to forgive ourselves and others while we are still in this earthly state. We can then help those we have hurt before we have to face ourselves on the next plane.

It is through coming to know ourselves that we learn to know our true source. We are our own creators. We create every dot and iota of our own lives. If we make mistakes, or learning experiences, as we often term them, there is an immutable law which cannot be changed, which gives us all the time we need to learn to overcome them. We will eventually learn that only love is truth. We are ever evolving. What we don't learn in one lifetime, will be learnt in another. It doesn't matter how long it takes. We are on a path back to the God-head, and whether we know it or not, whether we accept it or not, it is inevitable that we will find our true Source.

At each point in our life we face challenges and change. I was told each turning point is another challenge, another chance to grow. When life begins to lack the challenge it is time to wind up and move on. Following the guidance of our intuition is the wisest path to follow. We may not know what is around the corner but each step will be revealed to us in time. We are told to take one step at a time and trust in the universe.

> *You are about to enter a new phase in your life, and if you take this wonderful opportunity for growth that is being opened up to you, you will find it leads you into the depths of your heart's desire. .*
>
> *. . . Take all things in your stride and one day they will be looked upon as the greatest treasures life could give you. These things are in themselves unpolished jewels to be transformed into the most dazzling beauty you could ever imagine. These lights of beauty are waiting to be revealed to you. The promises of the future go with you.*

Only *we* hold the key to escaping further re-births. Only *we* hold the answer to our prayers. Only by our earnest desire to seek recompense for things we have done, for which we will have regrets now, or in the spirit life to come, can we win the Grace of God and learn our lesson. Our life lesson is to learn to love. It is to learn to accept everything that comes into our life with total unconditional love. It is through interaction with others, and service to others, that we learn this understanding.

Chapter 10

COMPLEXITIES IN INTERACTIONS WITH OTHERS

IN EVERY SITUATION WE FIND ourselves in this life with another human being, there is always an exchange of energies. One is always competing for energy from another whenever there is a confrontation between two or more people. This energy exchange is so subtle at times, we are not even aware of it. When we are angry or upset, we draw energy from another, and unless we are centred, we are unknowingly sapped of our energy through either a reaction of anger, or through pity.

When we come into contact with other human beings; which without there would be no growth; we are always facing some type of interaction, conflict or energy exchange. We have to learn to recognise the exchange that is taking place, and not surrender our energy to others when they are trying to manipulate our energy for their own purposes. We have to stay centred within our own centre and name the situation for what it is. Only through total unconditional love can we learn to overcome this manipulation.

There always seems to be a competition for energy on this planet. Even when one feels love toward another human being, he or she can still become drained of energy. As the one receiving the love becomes more uplifted, the other usually feels tired and drained. That is the way it seems to go all the time in the play of life. Our energies fluctuate up and down and back and forth between others. When people are in love they often look outside of themselves for the love from the other person, instead of taking that energy from Divine Source and keeping centred. They think the love is from another, when it actually comes from within them. They then drain themselves by giving their energy away.

The energy from Source is unlimited, but we have to realise that it actually comes from our Source, and thereby flows through us, and is not from a limited source which can be depleted. This way we come to realise that there is no reason to fear the loss of this love, as there is always an unlimited abundance of it all around us. It is important, however, to surround ourselves with white light if we are in a place where there are many people, as often others can drain our energy just by being around us. This is sometimes called psychic vampire attack. If we are ill or depressed, this is most likely to affect us. Therefore we have to protect ourselves with the white light.

When another person is angry, and we react, anger swells up in us. The ego is always threatened by another's anger, unless we become aware of our own power to control all our thoughts. Our little egos are only too easily upset if we feel rejection or hurt from another's actions. What we are actually doing in this situation is giving our energy away to that other person. They may not even be aware of this energy exchange, but it is always on a constant flow back and forth between personalities at all times. Wherever there is conflict, you will find an energy exchange. Wherever there is distress, or even compassion between people, you will find an energy exchange. Wherever there is an exchange of passion in any situation, there will be energy being moved.

I tried to overcome my feelings of negativity and annoyance which were weighing me down. I was told:

> *When you let feelings of anger and negativity overtake you; you are creating an environment or negativity to grow within you. You are sending out feelings of negativity— even if others are unaware of it on a conscious level—and*

creating a situation for yourself which will cause all this negativity to flow back to you!

To prevent this from happening, you must recall in each moment, that only love is real, and only love will keep you centred. Do not react in any situation. Allow yourself to simply go quiet within, and draw on your inner strength. Let bygones be bygones.

Do not try to hold onto a situation which has caused you hurt or pain. Simply let it go and tell yourself that this was a very valuable lesson and one which you appreciate for its opportunity for your growth. Simply allow. Let others learn their own lesson. Advise others, if necessary, with kindness and compassion.

Let your inner self be in control. Go within your heart centre. Remain balanced and allow love to flow through you. You cannot image the wonderful outcome a little bit of love and compassion can achieve.

There is nothing wrong with compassion, but we must not let it become sympathy which tends to make us feel drained and tired. The difference is that compassion is love being poured out from our divine Source, and which fills us with more energy. Sympathy is an outpouring from our limited ego, when we see others as the body only. Because we see it from the ego, it drains our energy pattern, as we limit the flow from divine Source by not being aware of the situation from the higher perspective. Compassion rises above sympathy as it sees from the whole person. It recognises the other as being divine. It is important for us to maintain our balance of energy by seeing life as being integrated and all things happening for divine purpose.

Our purpose in this life is service to our fellowman. We must however, remain centred, and give of ourselves with unconditional love. Judgement drains us. We are far better if we can remain in a state of non-judgement and acceptance, giving from our Source. This way we can maintain the balance of love because we are treating each being we encounter as if they are, themselves, a god-being, and equal in every way to ourselves. We then feel oneness with everybody we come in contact with, and find we can maintain our balance because we have self-love within ourselves.

Energy is the substance that makes up life. Unless we understand, however, what is happening all the time, we cannot control our moods and our actions. It is only through controlled thought and being aware of what is transpiring at all times, that we can have control over our lives and maintain it in any situation. It is up to us to act rather than react in any situation.

The energy around this planet is unlimited. There is a source of energy available to everyone. This is available to be tapped into without any loss or drain. It is only through using the energy from this Greater Source that we can stay in control of a situation without depleting our own, or another's, energy. Once we realise this source is available, and know that within ourselves is the power to control this energy, we cannot be caught off guard. It is through this awareness that we come to realise our own unlimited power.

Sometimes we play the victims, sometimes the rescuers, and sometimes the manipulators or dominators. Throughout life we are caught up in this energy exchange. Even as little children we are subconsciously demanding attention, and taking energy for our own purposes. Every time there is interaction between two or more people, there is always a power struggle. The only way we can overcome this, is by releasing the need to control, the need to have power over others. We have to learn to observe everything that comes to us, without reacting. We have to look at life and watch it unravel without trying to control it. We have to trust in the universe, and know that whatever happens is for our highest good. We do not have to control. We can then use our free will to act, rather than re-act.

How many times do we pick up feelings or thoughts of another person? Have you ever been thinking of someone, and at that exact moment the phone will ring and it will be them? Have you ever been experiencing a particular journey in your mind, and then you find out later that someone you know was actually there at the time you were visualising it? It can also happen that one experiences the *feelings* of others when they are in close proximity to them.

These things are happening all the time, more and more, as the consciousness of the planet is awakened. We are picking up psychic connections to others. It is not an unusual experience, reserved for the very special or psychic people. It is something everyone can and does experience at one time or another. This will begin to happen more, as people open up to the universe and release their old control patterns. By letting go of the need to control, we are opening our psychic channels and being more open to experiences like synchronicity, or what some might call coincidences. There are no coincidences. Everything that comes to us is part of the greater plan of the universe. If we surrender to the energy of the universe, we can tap into the power which is the knowing of all things.

Control and surrender are at opposite ends of the pole. We cannot do both. If we try to control every situation, we are blocking the natural flow of energy. The only way to let go of this control is to say: "I surrender everything to the universe. Guide me and direct me through this situation."

One of the things that, ironically enough, forces us to lose control is panic. We are caught up in a web of dread, affliction, trepidation, hysteria, and chaos. Control slips away from us. Yet it is through a situation of total panic, if we totally surrender because our fear is so great we feel we have nothing else to lose, the ego gives over to a higher consciousness and we find ourselves in a state of expanded awareness. It is from this vantage point that we can see the wonder and the beauty of existence that we were never aware of before.

Knowing this divine Source exists is the first step. Once we have realised this, and have a personal connection to it, it is easier to come back to this point whenever we feel conflict or disharmony in our lives.

As divine guidance says:

> It is truly pleasing to see such joy upon your world. There is, however, much sorrow. Many who show outward joy are feeling insecure and lonely within. This is the time for

ones of your planet to come to the child within and love that part of themselves that they have neglected. This is a great opportunity for self understanding. Joy does not come from outside possessions or from those outside oneself. It comes from truly loving self and finding the joy within one's own heart.

When you look at someone, look deep within their eyes and shower your love upon them. You are seeing parts of self that you have not understood or acknowledged. Those you see in your dreams which cause you distress; are the parts of self you have not acknowledged. These can be healed through being embraced and accepted, taken to the heart and given love. They are not your enemies. They show you reflections of what is within. Let them come forward to the light and know that nothing can harm you. All beings are interconnected on many levels. Without this connection life would be stagnant, wither and die. Life exists because it is connected. Accept all as part of the whole.

The world is in need of understanding this connection. Look within and understand the complexities within self first, then the complexities within nature and within all of humanity will be understood. When you can understand self, you will see that others also are just reflections of self and are helping to bring these complexities to the light by reflecting unresolved parts of self back to you.

Learn first to understand self and these reflections will no longer be needed. Then truly peace on earth can occur. It does not come from outside of self but from within. Learn the lessons of accepting and loving all of self first. Be in peace this day. We leave you in love. We are also part of you . . .

Chapter 11

CHAPTER 11

FORGIVENESS

FORGIVENESS IS THE BALM TO humanity's woes. Without forgiveness, humankind would not be able to progress towards his eventual enlightenment. Forgiveness is not easy. We need to understand what we need to forgive. If we can understand our own journey, we will begin to understand others, and what they need to experience. Once we have done that, we will be on our way towards forgiving ourselves as well as others. Lack of forgiveness is holding up the spiritual progress of the human soul. It is the major cause of every problem humanity has ever faced, lifetime after lifetime. It results in most of the illnesses we face, as we harbour them within our bodies. It causes disagreements and dissatisfaction through not seeing that what we perceive in others is actually a part of our own make-up that we have not acknowledged. It brings mistrust and misunderstanding on a greater scale than one could ever imagine. It is non-forgiveness that causes most of our anger and resentment.

I have felt anger and frustration many times in my life. Usually it is a time when I am refusing to face the real obstacle that this occurs. I might feel anger at another because I am asked to do something I do not want to do at that time. I may be busy doing something else, and the anger just springs up because I am annoyed at being interrupted. I have come to recognise that this is because I have not allowed myself to understand their point of view. I have been totally engrossed in my own work and have found it hard to pull my mind away to follow instructions. This creates a frustration and searing of my own feelings because I cannot express myself. I feel I cannot forgive the interruption at the time. This is only a small example. There are many times I have felt so angry that I feel I cannot forgive others. Yet if we reflect on it, it is usually something *we* are not facing that causes this anger.

On reflection of our life, we see that most of the time this non-forgiveness is of ourselves. Many of the repressed feelings that have been hidden all our lives are now coming to the surface to be healed. All these repressed emotions and feelings need to see the light in order for them to be finally cured.

It appears that every secret is coming out into the open to be revealed. The Bible said "nothing shall be hidden from their eyes". There will come a time when we will no longer be able to have any secrets. Our auras will reflect any feelings we have, and others will be able to read them.

The sexual indiscretions we are now hearing of some of the church leaders may well be the fact that they have been sexually deprived throughout their lives. It may be that deprivation in any form is unbalanced, and the soul searches for that balance in ways that are not 'politically correct'. We cannot condemn anyone unless we understand where they are coming from, but we can realise that these things are now being brought into the light. In the case of the priests, this could well be because they have deprived themselves of sexual union all their lives, and are trying to find their life's experience through whatever means they can. Incidentally it is through sexual expression that the human soul can find its true expression of self. Priests have denied themselves for years, by being celibate, and yet this is not the way the Creator intended it. We were always meant to experience sexual union as a beautiful experience between souls.

Many of our feelings of guilt revolve around sex. This has been inbred into our society for decades. This was always meant to be a natural form of expression, has been dirtied and made to be ugly by the church. Yet we do need to understand ourselves, and it is through a natural expression of orgasm through sexual intercourse that this journey towards the self is leading us. We must find the means within ourselves to forgive any and all of the feelings of guilt we have carried throughout our lives regarding sex. Understanding ourselves is half the battle. We have to write a new slate for ourselves. Forgiveness is our pathway towards releasing our negative feelings and finding the unconditional love within.

We have all faced lifetimes where we have made contracts with God. We have been everybody within our experiences. We may have made contracts not to marry, or not to own money. We may have agreed to experience the negative side of emotions in order to learn what it was like. The cellular memory remembers. We are now being given the opportunity to release these emotions, as they no longer serve us. We have reached a stage in human evolution where we now have the opportunity to accept the new energy we are being offered and take up the mantle of self-forgiveness and renewal. Forgiveness is the first step towards self-love. Self-forgiveness is the key to the kingdom. It not only opens the door. It is the hinges on the door and the key to the door. Self-forgiveness is the first lesson in reaching that wonderful being who is our Greater Self: the being that is our own Angel within us. Once we release any negative feelings we have, we find the unconditional love within.

When we fail to forgive another, we are actually seeing something that we cannot forgive or accept within our own nature. It may be something we had done in the past and cannot forgive ourselves for, or even remember, as we have pushed it so far back into our minds. Or it may be something deep within our soul, for which we feel guilty, carried over from another, or other, lifetimes, and it is still there today, deep within our cellular memories.

The bottom line is, whenever we feel something like this: a withdrawing, or a withholding of our feelings, we can always be sure that it is *something* that we haven't faced within ourselves that is triggering this feeling and holding us back. When we pass from this life, one thing that can hold us back from our eventual meeting with the light is the tightening feeling of non-forgiveness. When we refuse to forgive another, you can be sure that there is always an element of something within ourselves that we are refusing to face.

The only way we can stop this blockage and face the person, or overcome the feelings within ourselves, is to forgive them. Even if we are not consciously aware of what we are doing, it is by letting go; completely letting go of this feeling of tightness that enfolds us; that we begin towards the path of forgiveness not only of others; but most importantly of all; of ourselves.

There is always some underlying feeling within ourselves that needs to be dealt with, when we have this tightness. *To forgive is divine*—this is one of the great teachings of the Masters. Forgiveness is the most gracious way towards reaching enlightenment as it is in so doing, that we reach a deeper understanding, not only of others, but of ourselves and our whole unified nature as part of creation.

Like everyone else who walks this planet in human form, I have many such feelings towards others. It is inevitable that we will have some times in our life's experiences where we find we are holding back, withdrawing, or blocking what is coming. We find that we cannot face certain people. It may be something they should have done, or something that they haven't done that we feel they should have done. It may even be a feeling of conflict, anger, or animosity that we feel towards them. We do not know why, and yet the feeling is there. They may have done something that we are consciously aware of, or it may even be something that we just sense, without knowing why.

Journey of Our Souls

Our souls are not new to physical life. Most of us have had many lifetimes on different planets, as well as on planet earth. We have lived on planets within this solar system as well as in other systems many light years away. Some have had lives on Venus or Mars before they were made inhabitable to our life forms, and also on another planet, which was destroyed many millions of years ago, and is now part of an asteroid belt. We learnt many things through our previous lives. When we look back and see why we did certain things, and understand ourselves, then we will see why others are also experimenting and learning from their own experiences.

We began our existence as sparks of living energy. These sparks were innocent souls. We came to experiment. Much of the learning of the arts evolved on Venus. But there grew a time when those souls learned to discriminate between themselves and those less fortunate. This created vanity, pride, bitterness and separation. Through a string of varied circumstances, fear of those who were different from us was infiltrated into our souls.

Those that lived on Mars learnt communication and survival skills. But they also learned to fight. They learned about war. They carried over their pride, greed, and bitterness, from previous lifetimes. In time they remembered many of the experiences from earlier lifetimes. Those experiences included helplessness at an inability to help others. This occurred almost at a point in their evolution where they were ready to move to a higher vibration. They had agreed to accept these souls to their planet as they felt they were ready to help them. They found the challenge too difficult and unfortunately they became confused, frustrated, and discouraged. It had the effect of blocking their further evolution and many did not evolve as they might have done.

The hardest part of growing for these souls, however, was the blockage that they had carried over from other lives: that of non-forgiveness. The memory cells held all their experiences from previous lives within these new bodies. They found it too hard to really forgive themselves for their failed efforts. This is where most of the problems of these souls really began, as they had great difficulty forgiving themselves, and yet they did not even consciously remember why!

We have to understand how forgiveness relates to our souls. We have lived many, many lives and sometimes the cells of our bodies carry memories from other existences that we have blocked.

Rebirth or Reincarnation

Reincarnation has often been misunderstood. Many people have thought it means that the personality of the soul incarnates again, but it is not quite like that. Once a soul has passed over, that segment, or aspect, of the soul that lived, does not "come back" again. A soul is whole in its entirety, and only a portion of a soul will incarnate in a body at the one time. The particular facet of the diamond that comes to experience life again is another facet of the soul that still needs to be polished.

If we could imagine the soul as a complete book, each page being a year in the life of that soul. All the pages follow one another, as each year follows another. Each chapter represents one lifetime. All the pages connect to make the chapter that is one lifetime. Each chapter is a different lifetime. Some are shorter, others are longer. All the chapters have to connect in some way, but they are all different, yet each chapter is separate by itself. This is what our soul's journey is like. Each lifetime we experience a different *part* of our soul's particular journey and learn a different set of experiences.

During the time when the Christ walked the Earth, it was accepted that re-birth was a given among the some groups of Jews, the Gnostics and the Essene Community. The Essenes were discovered when the Dead Scrolls were uncovered and many believe now that a lot of Jesus' teachings came from them. Unfortunately it was written out of the pages of our Holy Book sometime in the fourth century. It was then that the feminine energy was taken out of the church, and male dominance ruled. There are many reasons this was done, but the most predominant one was that the church wanted to maintain power over the populace. If the people were free to realise that they could re-experience life again in another body after they died, then they would not be beholden to the church. Fear was then the tool to hold people in obedience to the church authorities.

Karma, or repaying for our wrongs, is not a punishment. Rather it is a form of choosing to make up for something we feel we have failed to do, or that we have done wrongly. There is no right and wrong, for all is a learning experience. One of the greatest forms of learning, however, is learning to forgive ourselves for any oversight or for anything we feel we have not done right. The law of karma is cause and effect. Whatever we send out will inevitably come back to us. Whatever feelings we hold onto, even if it is fear of something, will be always drawn back to us.

The act of forgiving is learning to have faith that what we need is already accomplished as we let go of prejudices, judgments, grudges, and selfish feelings. There can be no greater healing for humanity, or for the planet itself, than that of forgiveness. When people of the world forgive themselves, and release their past; peace for everyone will surely follow. Forgiveness is total acceptance and letting go of all, or any, of our past that we are still holding onto. If we cannot forgive, we are blocking the natural flow of life, and preventing our lives from moving forward. Likewise, we are also blocking the movement of the planet herself to move onward towards its transition.

Many of us do not even realise that we are blocking our energies, or why. We may be holding a grudge against somebody, or even feel we cannot forgive ourselves. We may feel that a loved one who has passed on does not forgive us and we feel guilt, as it may be *us* that we cannot forgive. It is imperative, if we are to move onwards towards the awakening of our souls, that we learn to forgive ourselves. We have to see ourselves for who we really are. It is time for us to wake up and remember who we are. It is time for us to wake up and remember why we came here. And it is time for us to wake up and forgive our brothers and sisters, and our selves. We are not who others see us as, or even as we think we are ourselves. We are far more than that. We are a child of God, a spark of divine—a being of light. We are, in fact, in everything that is around us.

I have often wondered who I really am. I have had countless experiences with so many different people, and to each I was a different person. I am a mother to my children, a wife to my husband, a friend to my friends, an employee, a co-worker, a daughter to my parents, a sister to my siblings, etc. To each of these relationships I am a different person, and they, no doubt, all see me differently. But I am none of these. In reality I have a vast multi-dimensional soul that experiences many things. So do you. If we can see how minute this part of us really is, we will see that holding grudges against somebody is just wasted energy. To let go and let God is really all we need to do.

We are beautiful beings of light. We cannot perceive this most of the time, because we are so caught up in this world with all its troubles, fears, diseases, and impurities. Yet this is our true essence. I asked the question of my guides *"Who am I?"* I received the following.

> *You are the wonder of all that you see around you. You are the beauty of the ocean, pounding upon the shore; you are the beauty of the peace that the ocean is; you are all that you see and so much more. You have the gift of physical life. This is only a portion of who you are. Do you not notice all around you that people are changing? They are being affected by the awakening of the earth herself in myriads of ways. The earth is reflecting back mankind's own responses, with great upheavals throughout the whole planet.*
>
> *Can you not notice the politics of the world changing? These are but one of the many subtle differences. Your economic system is another. These are reflections of what is happening within the changing soul of mankind—the changing perceptions of man.*
>
> *As humankind questions within the rightness or wrongness of his own life, so too will these responses be reflected outward by your Mother Earth. All is one. And what happens within the mind of man strongly affects the outward reactions of the planet. You are not separate and never were. All is happening through the changing perceptions of man, and the questioning that is going on all around you . . .*
>
> *. . . For all those who suffer, your peace is assured, as you come to the understanding of who you are, and why you*

are here. You have chosen this path for your own glory and your own learning of life. This is an honoured thing to do.

For all those who are finding stress in your life, you are also blessed. For the answer to your yearnings for peace is only a step away. You have this glory and beauty, awaiting you as you step into your new day. Go with peace and know you are blessed.

We really must release the stress in our lives by learning to forgive, beginning with ourselves. When we have learned the lesson of forgiveness within ourselves, we will find that all the anger, hurt, jealousy, pride, and hatred we ever felt towards another human being, will just dissolve. If we can just do it once, we will find that the next time is easier, and the next time easier again. We will find that there is no more animosity against anyone, when we have learned to forgive at the very core of the problem: within our own selves, of ourselves. When we truly love our Selves, our Greater Selves, we cannot hold a grudge against another. We will see things in a new light. We see in them a reflection of ourselves, and when we release any negative feelings about ourselves, then they will mirror back to us who we truly are.

Understanding who we are is important in seeing the reasons behind much of what we feel. Many of us are carrying ancestral karma. Some are here in this lifetime to heal many generations of karma from our fathers and forefathers. This is why the ego is having such a battle. When we begin to transform our inner feelings, we release *all* karma from all of our lives and of those of our family who went before us. This is why so many are feeling burdened by all that is happening to them. When we transform karma through forgiveness, this brings forgiveness through all generations of our family history. Fear of the ego being lost (separation) is causing people to fear. But the opportunity for learning and growth for many generations past is here for us this lifetime if we can let go of the ego and forgive others, and realise we are all one. If we allow resentment and non-forgiveness to damage our souls, we will not be able to move forward with the planet when it raises its vibration and transitions into the new age.

Negative Thoughts

I believe that negative thoughts are like weeds. If they are allowed to grow they multiply and are very hard to get rid of. They have to be constantly monitored and pulled out. The best thing we can do is to get rid of them all as soon as we are aware of them, and replace them with thoughts of compassion, kindness and sharing, and allow our light to shine on all without exception. Just by acknowledging our thoughts, or observing them, we will soon be able to release them altogether. Just watch yourself next time you feel anger toward another. What is really going on in your mind? Can you find it in yourself to forgive yourself for the anger, and to forgive the target of that anger?

One of the things that have caused this planet to deteriorate so fast is humankind's greed. Greed is based on a feeling of fear of not enough. But if we could but realise it, life is eternal. We live in a universe of unlimited prosperity, and there is no need for us ever to feel fear of poverty or lack. We have everything given to us by spirit that we could possibly want. Thoughts of greed and want only come about when we start to let fear enter our lives. This fear causes us to feel guilt. Our soul knows its own perfection and knows that there *is* nothing to be guilty of. We must allow ourselves to be forgiven for any, and all fear based feelings we have ever had.

The area around the Middle East holds a lot of negative energy. Only by sending healing energies to this area, to soothe the burning hatred and anger that is presently rife in the Middle East, will we be able to assist these tortured souls to forgive one another. The most important thing for these souls is to be understood before they can be forgiven. We really do have to "walk a mile in another man's shoes" before we can begin to understand where they are coming from. Most of those living in this area have been brought up from young children to fight. They don't know anything else. How can they learn to understand themselves as beings of light if the world continually refuses to forgive them and is constantly fighting them?

Forgiveness is such a hard thing to do sometimes. I have found that it is preferable in some circumstances to not try so hard to forgive, as this just puts more energy in the place where it is not needed. Sometimes if we just let go and not allow resentment to fester, things will dissolve by themselves. It is better to completely release others than try to forgive, if we find forgiveness too hard. That way we take away the energy that has caused the problem in the first place. The collapse of the Berlin wall came about, not through forgiveness, but through total apathy. Those who were on either side of the wall just lost interest in why it was there in the first place. Maybe that is the best thing we can do, if we find it difficult to forgive someone. Maybe just losing interest is the answer. By releasing hold on something or someone, we let it go.

It has been proven that the hundredth monkey syndrome works. This began when some monkeys living on an isolated island were given potatoes that were covered with sand. One monkey began to wash his potato in the sea to get off the sand, and one by one all the monkeys began doing it. On the mainland many miles away other monkeys suddenly began doing the same thing, and before long monkeys everywhere seemed to be doing the same. This is called the critical mass. This is why prayer and healing work, particularly when sent by a group of people as it is multiplied many-fold. The energy created through mass prayer or meditations is very strong. If one person joins with another the strength of the prayer is much stronger. As more join in, the affect can be far reaching. We were told: "If two or more gather in my name, I will be there" . . . We *can* affect others by our thoughts and feelings and by our prayers. A small group sending healing can affect a whole country. The effect of the one affects the many.

If we can send feelings of love to those fighting in any war, it may help them to finally realise that love and forgiveness is the only answer to conflict. If we can send healing energies to heal through forgiveness, and somehow help those concerned to realise that war will only stop when one forgives another, then the affect will reach many more, and we will be assisting the world to find peace. It is the soldiers who do the fighting, not the heads of state.

It takes each individual to awaken within himself. We do not need to be controlled by the heads of government.

The song "Universal Soldier", written in the 1960's by Buffy Sainte-Marie, comes to mind:

> "He's the universal soldier,
> And he really is to blame.
> His orders come from far away no more.
> They come from here and there, and you and me,
> And brother don't you see,
> This is not the way we put an end to war . . ."

It goes on to say,

> "He's the one who gives his body
> As a weapon of the war
> And without him all this killing can't go on . . .
> He's the one who must decide who's to live and who's to die
> And he never sees the writing on the wall."

When each man on earth thinks for himself, humankind will have a chance to put an end to war. The light directed by us to just one soldier, has an effect more far reaching than we could imagine.

Those light workers who are here on earth, people like Maryanne Williamson with her prayers of peace, and others, like James Twyman, who is singing peace prayers in all the war-torn parts of the world, are helping the earth tremendously. Time and again, Jimmy has gone to the war places: Ethiopia, Ireland, Bosnia, etc. and has asked for the assistance of prayers to go along with him as he sang his peace songs. As people joined him from all parts of the world, no matter where they were, things changed in those places. Miracles happened, and wars ceased. Did we ever think we'd see a black President in South Africa? Let alone a black President in the United States? Did we ever think that the Berlin Wall would just collapse, or that communism would cease in Russia, or peace would come to the bitterness in Ireland? The power of prayer cannot be underestimated. It is one of the strongest ways of bringing about positive change to the world.

We've been told that forgiveness is the balm of the soul. Without forgiveness we cannot move forward. Without forgiveness we cannot move towards ascension with our planet. Forgiveness releases the feelings of hate and injustice we have allowed into our minds. It soothes every ache in our heart. It releases any pent up anger or hatred we might have. It allows us to be a whole being, living within a planet of polarities, and yet holding forth our armour of love towards our fellow being.

Forgiveness has to begin on a small scale first. When we have conflict in families, we are told:

"It is therefore in parents and children forgiving each other for what they have not done that the Holy Spirit's lessons are learned. Each will have looked on the other, no longer to fulfil certain needs through specific roles, but as brother and sister who God has joined to walk forgiveness' path together . . ."

Forgiving begins with those closest to us: our family, friends, relations and neighbours. When we have learned to forgive, we allow our hearts to open to peace on the Earth, and we become free from the tightness and blockages that held us in their chains. We need not feel guilt any longer. We need not feel fear or animosity towards another fellow human being. When there is no resentment left in us, we can then become open and sharing. We will have begun the journey of healing ourselves and finding release and have become a master of our emotions. Maybe then, we will discover what powerful beings we really are.

Chapter 12

THE POWER WITHIN

W E HAVE BARELY BEGUN TO realise what powerful beings we really are. We so often shun our power, because we are afraid to show it. We keep it under a bushel, because we do not want it exposed to the light. We may *feel* powerless, but we are not. Our strength comes from within, and we have more than we could possibly imagine. No one is a victim. We only feel that way if we allow ourselves to be. We can overcome anything if we so choose.

Inner strength is not judged by outward appearances. The weakest person may have the greatest inner strength of all. They will battle all odds to overcome any adversary. They do not use physical strength as in the strength of a weight lifter, or a person of outer strength, but they show an inner strength, unsurpassed by any that show only brawn.

Mother Teresa showed remarkable strength. Although she was a small lady, she would go out into the streets of Calcutta and carry in dying bodies. These were people who no one else would touch because they were afraid of becoming infected. Her inner strength carried her through many, many years of working non-stop with sick people, healing them as best she could and comforting them. She empathised with those who suffered poverty and hunger and gave them food, understanding and love. She fought against all odds to live a long life of serving others.

An Australian, Ian Gawler, showed enormous strength when he walked from Adelaide to Melbourne. What is so amazing about this man is that he had suffered cancer and lost his leg. He managed to walk over 700 kilometres (over 420 miles) with one leg! His inner strength was so great and his determination so all-encompassing that he was able to achieve a feat many others would consider impossible! There are other great souls who have also shown such courage and strength in light of suffering.

Our inner strength comes from the heart, or the soul and our souls are so much more than we could even imagine. We have the power to create anything we desire. Even in our weakest moments, we can find this strength within. I have often felt incapable of finding any strength to overcome the all-powerful feeling of defeat, and entrapment. But I was told that we have the strength within us to overcome anything. Even in our weakest moments, we have more strength than we can possibly imagine. We have great power within our inner souls, as we are one with the Divine Source itself.

We often do not acknowledge this, as we are afraid of what others will think if we show our inner strength. We are afraid they will think we are too bold, or too outspoken, or too proud. But this hidden power is within each of us. When Jesus spoke to the wind and the waves, he was showing us that when we command the Higher Powers within us, we too, can speak to the elements of nature and command them in our power.

I often do not feel like I am powerful. I often feel like I have no control of a certain situation. I feel helpless. Yet we are told:

> *Your strength within comes from being who you really are, not by listening to others. Be charitable to others and listen quietly to their advice, but then go within to your own feelings and abide by what you feel. Trust in your own inner knowledge.*
>
> *Many before you have fallen through trying to please another and not listening to their inner voice. Hold to your own, and you will never be disappointed. You have far more strength within than you realise. I leave you now. Another comes to talk with you.*

There is much power within you, but you have hidden this power for fear of it being known to others. You have been afraid of your power, because you have misused it in times past. Now is the time for this power and your brightness, to shine for all to see. The world has a great need of it. Many of my legions are now upon the earth plane, and many are being awakened now. This reminder is for all who feel the tug of compassion in their heart. Your time is now.

Do not fear for your future. You write your own future. You write it with fear or with love. Let not others persuade you away from your true lesson—the calling which you feel in your hearts. The purpose you came here to do is now being called upon. Rise up and claim your power—your birthright—your light. You are my children. You are stars of the Creator. And your time for revealing this has now come.

Stand in your power. Be who you are. I bless you and give you courage in this time of need. So be it.

We are being told by Spirit that it is now our time to stand up and be counted. Our time for holding back has passed. It is now time to release all past that does not serve us, and move forward. The world is waiting for us. It is waiting for us to emerge into our true selves, and be who we were always meant to be. It is time now for us to stand in our power and face the world the way we were always meant to face it.

We feel powerless so often, when we become sick. Yet we do not realise at the time that we do have the power to overcome sickness of any kind. We often choose a certain condition to learn a particular lesson. When we can come to understand that everything is alive, even inanimate objects from computers to cars, as they all have living elementals, or spirit, within them we have the power to create anything we desire. We can ask the spirit in our car to look after it, and it will. I knew a man once who used to do just this. He was a great teacher. One day he drove his car into the garage for a service and the garage mechanic told him it was a wonder the car got him anywhere as it was in such a bad condition. He did not tell the mechanic that he had asked for the little spirit in the car to look after it for him and keep it going! He also taught me that we have the power to ask for whatever we need to be there *before we need it* and it always is. I have tried this and it really does work! It only has to be said once and then forget it. Spirit never forgets our request.

We can send love to our computers and they will respond by not crashing on us. How many of us, in moments of anger and frustration, have had the computer crash on us? You can bet it always happens when we are in a bad mood. Have you ever wondered why? It is the thoughts we send out that attract a like vibration. We can focus thoughts of love on anything around us, and it will respond in kind. Inanimate objects have the ability to communicate to us the physic energy they pick up from things around them. It is entirely possible that in years to come, we will be able to pick up the energy of an object. Each object has a level of vibration of its own. As we become more in tune with nature and more sensitive to things around us, we will find we can hear these objects speak to us.

Death cannot harm us. It is just a passing through into another dimension, and back again to experience life. We eventually attain the higher dimensions of such great light that we no longer need to incarnate again in physical form. We can take with us whatever we desire for our own potential and our own growth. We *do* choose however what we take with us in each lifetime, and that which is intended for our highest purpose. We come here with a mission: a life plan and it is our guides that help to prompt us to carry it out.

We have the power to create our own future. We so often let worries about the future or fears about the past overtake us. Our future reactions are based on what we have experienced in the past. We need not be afraid of what our future will hold as we write our future in each now moment. We must not let fear overtake us and drag us down. We have to lift our energies by being positive in our every moment:

My guides have said:

Do not let feelings of despair, fear or gloom overtake you. These vibrations do not lift the earth. They hold her down like a chain net, which cannot be broken. Lighten your thoughts—do not let fear enter your mind and heart.

By allowing all, you are accepting all into your heart, and not restricting your movements by fear-driven feelings and thoughts. These feelings place a lock, or blockage, on your emotions, which stop the love from flowing through your veins.

When you relax you will be surprised at the difference it makes to your vibration. You actually slow right down and become one with the things around you. As you do this, if you could see into the etheric world, you would see streams of coloured lights spinning off you and onto every item that catches your vision. It is a most beautiful sight from where we sit in the spiritual realm. The colours that radiate from you are most magnificent.

As you travel through your day, be in tune with the inner feelings you have about things that come into your day. As you experience each feeling, let it pass through you, and observe how you feel. Do not try to take this feeling to your heart. Rather let it pass through you and watch it travel on its way. You are beyond these feelings and far more than you could possibly realise.

If you look around you at the presence of others, you will see their angelic presences and know that they reflect your angelic presence also. Everything you see and feel has a connection to you in some way. By living and allowing all to pass without judgement of it, you are becoming a lighter person, and raising your consciousness towards a heightened vibration. As you raise your vibrations, you also lift the vibrations of the planet you walk upon, and each time you do this, you are assisting in her birth towards her new consciousness. Remember these words as you carry on into your day. They are for all people.

If we can use our problems and illnesses as opportunities to think about how to change our lives, we have power. Taking responsibility for ourselves is one of the greatest powers we have. Many people come through catastrophic illnesses saying it was the most wonderful thing that ever happened to them because it gave them a chance to see their lives differently. In my case, the loss of my daughter was a catalyst for me finding myself and awakening to the strength within me.

If, on the other hand, we feel we are victims, we will find it hard to find our power within. So often we feel intimidated by others, or we feel that we just can't do what we know we ought to do. It is not an easy thing to face the strength within us and move forward. But in order to break our pattern of powerlessness, we must accept the responsibility of our own power.

Nelson Mandala, the late African leader, wrote in his inaugural speech in 1994:

> "Our deepest fear is not that we are inadequate. Our deepest fear is that we are powerful beyond measure. It is our light, not our darkness, that most frightens us. We ask ourselves, who am I to be brilliant, gorgeous, talented and fabulous? Actually, who are you not to be? You are a child of God. Your playing small does not serve the world. There is nothing enlightened about shrinking so that other people won't feel insecure around you. We are born to make manifest the glory of God that is within us. It's not in some of us, it's in everyone. And as we let our own light shine, we unconsciously give other people permission to do the same. As we are liberated from our fear, our presence automatically literates others."

We serve nothing in the plan of ascension if we hide who we are. We have lived so long as victims that we are now afraid to own who we are. We have power within us beyond our wildest dreams. Our power is to be used for the good of all. Often in the past, in previous lifetimes we have had this power and have used it wrongly, and it has caused disastrous consequences to all concerned. We may have been given much authority, and abused it, and this is the reason why we now hide the power that is within us; because we are afraid of repeating a past mistake. Our souls know the reason we have hidden it for so long. But we have learnt from our past, and it is now the time to allow it to come into its own.

Through regression, Dolores Cannon discovered one of her subjects had a past where he'd tried to help another planet. He saw himself fitted with space outfit landing on a planet that he'd tried to assist. Through his intervention however, he'd interfered with the indigenous people of the planet and prevented their growth as it should have happened naturally. In this, his current lifetime, he was afraid to allow himself any power for fear he would repeat his past mistake. I think we all have similar fears for holding back our power.

Those who use power for selfish purposes will not survive in the new age. Those who use sexual prowess, for example, to keep another in abeyance or servitude will no longer be able to use this as a means of power over others. Each person, knowing who he or she is, will be master of himself, and there will be no more victim-hood among humankind. We will not be allowed to claim our power upon this planet any longer if we are intending to use it for ill purposes. The God-Creator/Source/All-that-Is has seen it all happen before. Creator will not allow another catastrophe to occur upon this planet because of power abuses. The dark energies that are trying to hold their power will not survive.

Humanity will no longer be allowed to use these powers unless they are for the highest good of all. It is time to acknowledge our own powerful energies, and to use them for the good of the whole. Our power can be used in the most positive ways; to help others to see themselves for who they really are; to help others fight their depression; their lack of self-worth; their illnesses and their fears. So many souls are in need of hearing this at this time. Depression lives in the lower chakra of the body, so if we can lift our vibrations we can rid ourselves of this debilitating emotion.

The Power of Emotions

We find our emotions rocketing to and fro so often these days. We are always fighting them, trying to stay centred. These emotions, and the strength of them, can be frightening. The time has come to do some "spring cleaning" of our emotions, sifting through all the forgotten corners and coming to new realisations. It is time for crying those unshed tears and letting go of any remainders of unresolved emotional residue.

I would sometimes find anger coming to the surface. Simple things seemed to cause me to become irrationally angry. My husband braking his car when I was reversing behind him, and not giving me warning, causing me to go into work fuming one morning. Yet there is no logical reason why this should be so. The anger just welled up so unexpectedly, without rational cause. By releasing this anger, it has evaporated and is no longer within me. If we hold the anger in, it is more likely to cause us harm further down the track. It is anger, frustration, resentment, etc. that are the causes of most of the diseases of humankind that develop in old age. Even doctors and psychiatrists are now admitting that a deep hidden anger or resentment, over many years possibly causes cancer. We are so powerful we can do this to ourselves! We have to deal with the fear of this now, as the old approach will not work. We manifest these sudden illnesses almost instantly now, as our power has become more obvious and we are calling these things to us.

The strength within us may be staying hidden because we don't want to acknowledge it for fear of its power. We know, deep down at a soul level, that we have allowed our power to cause harm upon the planet before. We know its potential, and we are afraid to unleash it. If we allow it to be released by sending it love, accepting it, and acknowledging it, telling ourselves that it is okay to be angry, that it is okay to be emotional *as long as it doesn't hurt another,* then it will cease to be a problem for us. We can unleash our anger by hitting a pillow, or even walking the dog. Any feelings that we lock up inside us will inevitably come to light again as a physical disease at some stage later in our lives. If we allow our anger release, then the earth will transmute it and our other emotions, and we will find them being replaced by feelings of pure love.

The greatest power of all is that of self-love. This love will give us everything that we have ever needed. The power is within us through understanding our own potentials and our own inner selves.

James Twyman, a peace troubadour and author of the well-known book *Emissary of Love*, among other books, interviewed a little child by asking her about her ability to see psychically what others were thinking. She felt that the gift she had was the same as many children today have. This child demonstrated the use of telekinesis and showed her understanding of the minds of others. For his benefit, she focussed energy on a bud not yet in bloom, and within seconds the flower opened in front of his eyes. For her it was a minor accomplishment. She felt her purpose in being here was to show others that they also had this gift.

This child was aware of other children all over the world with the same gift whom she had never met. But her main concern was that people today are afraid of the power that they have within them. They are afraid that the power they have will make others see them differently. The power that can, and will, change the world is love. *Love* is the vibration that emanates all things to a higher vibration. It is through love of all things; even inanimate objects that can cause them to move without being touched. It is the energy of love that moves objects, hearts and minds toward a greater understanding. This is the power we have within us if we would only lose our fear and use what we have. If we do not use it correctly we can become ill.

We do have the power within to help the world. A great master has told us:

> "The greatest service you can render to mankind is to work truly and earnestly on the inner plane to radiate love and establish on the physical plane of life the thought,

the ideal, the feeling of brotherhood. Never waver in your belief that all is working together for the good of humanity. In the measure that you hold fast to this truth, so will you increase your power to help the world and all humanity? Preserve in your heart the strength of the spirit of Christ; give forth good thought—love thought. Humanity will absorb the light that you send forth. Instead of absorbing the dark and destructive forces, they will absorb the Light, the constructive, the Godlike, the Christlike qualities of life."

Power in Prayer

Miracles have been known to happen when we give power to prayer. Greg Braden, author of *The Isaiah Effect,* writes of a miracle where an elderly gentleman was strolling towards a parking lot and missed his footing with the metal cane as it collapsed and sent him crashing to the asphalt. He crumpled into a heap on the sidewalk while his wife screamed for help. Before he knew it, a woman was already there, cradling the gentleman's head in her hands. She gently moved the layers of skin around the neck to see where the bleeding was coming from. As she did so, she seemed to silently pray, as onlookers saw her looking towards the sky. They watched in amazement, as the open wound seemed to close. Moments later the ambulance arrived. They also traced the bloody marks on the skin and the clothing, only to find no wound there.

Braden talks about the power of mass prayer when, in November 1998, the effects of prayer were felt throughout the world as Iraq's time to end their war was upon them, and the military was in the process of firing on Iraq. At the very moment that countries around the world joined in this vigil, the president received a cease fire agreement. Is this a coincidence? Until we understand the intricacies of prayer, we will never know. He has discovered that prayer is not so much in the thought, or the words, but in the emotion, the *feeling and belief* of it already happening.

The earth is now raising its own vibrations, and unless we do the same, along with the planet, we will no longer incarnate upon the earth when our time is over. There have been other planets prepared for those who still wish to focus in third dimensional energies. Our planet will no longer be in a vibration to sustain the lower energies and must move on in its own evolution. One way of lifting our vibrations is to allow ourselves to feel gratitude for all things around us.

Chapter 13

UNDERSTANDING GRATITUDE

U NDERSTANDING GRATITUDE AND ITS PLACE in our lives is hard for many to believe. Many would not think gratitude had a place in world peace, but it does. Because everything around us is given to us freely by the earth herself, what she desires in return is humankind to be aware enough of her to thank her for the goodness and abundance she offers. The American Indians, the Australian Aborigines, and all the indigenous people of the planet knew this and have known it for hundreds and thousands of years. There is life in *everything*. That is why it is important to be grateful to everything that crosses our path, even inorganic objects, as they too have their life forms, even if we cannot see them.

Material and earthly abundance can only be achieved through a deep connection to Mother Earth. Abundance is the love and gratitude for what we have received. If there is no feeling of gratitude then the receiving is not as powerful, or fulfilling, as it could be. When we are free and allowing, we feel gratitude for everything that comes to us. We can be open and grateful for every little thing as if it were a gift from the universe. This way we begin to see what can be accomplished by the simple act of gratitude. When we offer blessings, we are giving to ourselves that which we wish to receive. Gratitude towards what we have is one of the surest ways to receive blessings without exception. We receive blessings as we give out gratitude. This is a natural law and one that is immutable. "For what we are about to receive, Lord make us truly thankful". This is a daily prayer for our food. This is like saying we have already received what we are expecting, and it is the right way to go about praying. If we pray like we already have what we are asking for, we are creating it already and are sure to receive it.

We don't really understand the power of prayer, or why it has such a strong affect on those things around us. When we pray with a deep heartfelt desire, we are actually causing our own cells to awaken to their true God potential. These cells connect to our subconscious, which hears our words and they likewise respond. I have been told many times that I only had to pray and my prayer would be answered. I seem to have a connection with the angels as my prayer is usually always answered for me. I can also send healing this way, through praying for people as those in spirit are only too ready to oblige.

Each morning when we step out of bed we have another new chance to begin again. We should never carry our worries and our distresses over from the day before. Each day is a gift in itself. We are alive. We have air to breathe. If we are lucky we have food and clothes. If we are even luckier we have a good job and a roof over our heads, and even a family or friends. Sometimes we forget just how lucky we are and how much we are blessed. Why should we fear for yesterday or tomorrow? Each day the sun shines for us, the air is fresh again, the sky is different, and the earth is newly awakened.

Despite the news of tragedies that surround us at times, there is always something to be grateful for. Even the smallest thing can make a huge difference, as we lift ourselves by our attitude, and it builds up our spirit. Each moment we are creating our own reality and our own world through the gift of gratitude. Our gratitude for the new day has a very large bearing on how we see the day, and how the day treats us. There is always something to be grateful for despite the state of our health. We have the opportunity at each sunrise, to change any thought, either negative or positive, that we have carried through from the previous day. Every little bit helps. If we are depressed and low, we attract those things of like to us, but when we lift our hearts, even a little, it can do so much for our morale and our spirit.

We don't realise what a great gift we are given by Spirit. If our gratitude is truly sincere, we have the addition of an extra gift, as everything we are grateful for, is given to us many times over. Every time we send gratitude for a blessing received, heaven takes the acknowledgment and doubles the blessing. Thus is the greatest gift of all is given to us.

The Indigenous peoples of the world knew how to give thanks. They were much closer to Mother Nature, as we were when we first came to earth, and they knew the importance of giving thanks for everything they took from the earth. They would give thanks to the vegetable or fruit before they plucked it from the earth. They would offer thanks for the life of the animal before they killed it. The Indigenous people did not just give thanks before eating, but before taking life. They were in touch with the vibratory construct of the planet itself. They *knew* how life worked, and that by giving thanks and gratitude, all things are lifted to a higher vibration.

The seer, Edgar Cayce, in a trance state, would see the molecules changing in the food as it was blessed. Holy water is water that is blessed so that the molecules change, thereby altering their composition and repelling anything of a negative nature.

The Australian Indigenous people have showed gratitude to the earth and their land by blessing it before the event of the Olympic Games in Sydney in 2002. This, to me, seemed a remarkable achievement and a wonderful gesture by the Olympic Committee. In fact, all of this grand event in Sydney, offered an opportunity, and indeed was received as such, for every country of the world to see how giving and sharing can bring about great things. It was gratifying to see the Australian Aborigines blessing the land in a ceremonial way, at the Opening Ceremony of the Games. I felt it was one sign that our world *is* changing, and that the consciousness of the planet, has indeed shifted.

In fact, with all the fears about the new millennium at the turn of the century, on the first of January 2000, it was gratifying to see the peoples of the world, all singing in joy at the beginning of a brand new era. It held quite a spell, watching such a momentous event on our television sets, and the world watched in excitement, and some trepidation, wondering what would happen. It became a joy to watch such enlightenment spreading across the face of the planet as people sang and danced in exultation.

The Indigenous people of the Americas, the Indians of America, would rise each morning and raise their hands to the sun, singing and dancing, and give praise for the new day. They would always give thanks for anything before they took it from the earth, and pray to the soul of the animal, thanking it for its life, before they took its life and killed it for their food. This was done in ceremonial ways.

Like the Australian Aborigines, the American Indians had members of each tribe who would not touch certain animals. Each of the people within various tribes had their own particular totem. I remember hearing a story of an Indian Chief who would never eat or kill buffalo. When he was old, his tribe left him in his tepee to die, as he was too old to continue to the warmer climate. One morning when winter was nigh, he was near starvation, and he came outside. There, lying in front of his tepee was a buffalo that had come to die. It had given its life for him to live; knowing it was going to die, in gratitude for his refusal to kill the buffalo!

Gratitude in Nature

We can see how gratitude works within nature. The birds wake each morning and sing in gratitude, then go about the task of collecting food for their young. They are never disappointed. Nature provides their every need. Every morning and evening the birds can tell us something. They sing every morning out of sheer gratitude to the new day. They do not hold anything back, but give it their all. Their songs actually cause the vibrations of the air to bring growth to the trees and plants. Have you heard of people telling you to sing to the plants?

Plants do respond to light-hearted sounds, and the bird song is one of nature's greatest gifts to the earth. It is the melodious sounds within the bird-song and the different notes that are sung, which cause change and growth in the plant kingdom.

The birds do not know where their next meal is coming from, but they sing in gratitude *for it*, knowing that they will be provided for. This reminds me of the time the Master spoke of the birds of the air; they do not toil, neither do they reap yet they are fed and clothed in all of nature's glory. They ask nothing but receive all, because they are grateful just to be alive.

The birds and animals also understand that gratitude for life is an assurance that what they need is already provided.

On gratitude, my guides have said:

> *Dear One,*
>
> *When gratitude fills a heart, it not only lifts the vibrations beyond the thought of the human form, but it actually opens the cells of the body and allows more light to enter in. It is the basis of creation. It allows all things to take place. You have read in your holy books that the angels in heaven are continually praising God. This is how life forms—through gratitude. love and gratitude are the things, above all else, that will lift mankind and create anew. They are what will raise the planet into a new vibration of light.*

When blessings and thanks are given for food before you eat it, the cells within the food actually respond and change, thereby altering their composition and creating a vital source of life and light, allowing light and life to enter the body when they are taken. Vegetation is alive and conscious, as well as the animals upon your earth. Each has a consciousness that understands Universal Law, and responds to gratitude, as it understands all things in their place. For when you eat foods with gratitude, you allow the life forms of that which is eaten to enter your system, thereby transforming its life into something else. It becomes another form of energy, which is another form of life. This is the cycle of change that is continually happening in nature, and one which you help to continue, by blessing all that comes to you in gratitude.

Gratitude opens the heart. It allows blessings to come pouring in. Have you not heard that when gratitude fills a heart, heaven takes the acknowledgment and doubles the blessing? This indeed is what happens. It is the law of giving and receiving. All that you give out is returned to you multi fold.

When you send blessings to others, you are opening the path for blessings to flow back to you. It is how all things flow within the Universal Law. Have you not noticed how we close our greetings to you with a blessing? Yes, my child, gratitude and blessing have great power, and are far more than mere words. They hold within them the very power of creation themselves. Bless you this day.

Blessing is a gift that we give ourselves. When we are open to thanking ourselves, we are open to receiving all that we ask for. It is indeed important to thank ourselves for the God within which is in all of us. If we send our prayers of thanks to others, we are in effect, giving our power away. By praying within to our Higher God Self, we are offering ourselves a double blessing. Blessings and gratitude actually open us to that part of ourselves which is called our Higher Self. True knowledge comes from knowing that the power of blessing our inner self, or Higher Self, is our greatest strength.

When we are grateful for what we have, we open a channel for more to come into our lives. If we go about our daily lives grumbling that we don't have this, and we don't have that, then nothing that we want will come to us. But when we go about our lives being grateful for all that we do have, we will find our paths open up, and all that we could ever desire will come to us.

By being grateful, we open the channels for all good things to flow back to us. We can even be grateful for the sad times and the times when we appeared to have nothing. For even in these times, we had opportunities given to us to expand and grow. The wisest men in the Chinese culture believe that when these sad times come it means good luck. They say that when we have our sad and bad times it means that we can only go upwards from here on.

The ancient act of tithing actually originated because it followed a universal law. By giving *freely* without any expectations in return, we open ourselves to receive from the universe. It is a universal law that what you give out comes back. When people were asked to give one tenth of their income and they did so freely, they could fully expect to receive ten times in return from the universe. Whatever we give, always comes back to us many times over. If it is food or clothing we are in need of, then we can be sure that what we give out in the way of material possessions, or even a kindness, will always come back to us, and usually just at the time we need it most.

I remember one story where a man driving along a highway late at night helped a stranded woman driver change a tire. This man was on his way back to his sick wife and three little children. He really didn't have time to stop but he did. Because of his kindness, he in turn was given a kindness when a neighbour came to the door and offered the family food and medical supplies. When we help others, it has a boomerang affect. The universe works in this way. We give in gratitude for what we have, and the more we give, the more we find others doing the same.

We do create what we want by the way we view ourselves. If we believe our income is limited, for example, then we have to ask ourselves who limited it? Our universe is an abundant universe. There is no lack within nature or within the universe. It is only our belief system that is limiting us. Everything that comes our way can be looked at as a gift in some way. We always receive from the universe what we need the most for our own growth. And remember it is we who asked for this on a soul level prior to this incarnation. The greatest tragedies of our lives can be looked on as stepping stones, or gifts, or catalysts to help us on our path forward in life. It is when we come to realise the gifts we have been offered that we have begun to understand how gratitude works. It opens opportunities for our further spiritual advancement.

Jesus once told a story about a man who was going away on a journey. He called his three servants together and to the first he gave five talents, to the second, two talents and to the third one talent, according to their abilities. While he was gone the servant with the five talents traded them and made five more. The servant with the two talents did the same and made two more, but the servant with the one talent buried it and hid it in the ground for fear of losing it. When the master returned he was impressed with the two servants who had doubled his money, but when he discovered the servant who had hidden his talent in the ground he was very angry. He took the talent from the servant and gave it to the one who had ten. In Jesus' words: "To him that has much, more will be given, but for him that has not, even what he has will be taken away".

A talent was a particular sum of money in those times. Jesus was showing us that if we are grateful for what we have, and use it wisely, we have more given to us. But if we refuse to make good with, or bury, what we are given, we lose it all.

I have heard of people who walk around telling everyone that they "don't have" this and they "don't have" that. They seem to be forever wanting, and are never satisfied. They may be ordinary people like you and me. They seem to be like us, but they are the type of people who wear you down because they are always complaining that they "don't have" what they want. They are the "have not" type of people. Then there are other people who appear to have little, yet you never hear them complain. They will be grateful for the small change they receive from their groceries. They will be grateful for the person who baked a cake for them. They will be even grateful for a small cup of milk, or being able to smell a rose. They are grateful for having seen a sunset. These people are the ones who believe they have everything they could ever want.

The difference in these two types of people is that the "have nots" are never grateful for what they do have. They always want more, and are never satisfied. The people who are so grateful for the small things are the ones who are always grateful for everything. Things just appear to come to them. Can you see the difference in these two types of people? When people are afraid that they "don't have" all the time, this causes so much resentment, that wars can start because of it. Why do you think wars begin in the first place? It is because the leaders of a particular country think that another country has more than them, and they want it.

From our smallest resentments and arguments, to the total futility of war, it all begins because one party wants what the other party has. But we *do* live in an abundant universe, and the sooner we can reconcile this idea in our minds, the sooner we will receive through our gratitude and the knowledge of this truth. What we believe we have, we manifest for ourselves. If we believe that we have all that we need, the universe provides all our needs for us. Others, who see this, think that they should have it, and may try to take it, causing more pain for both sides. Otherwise they might go about with resentment in their hearts. They may feel that what they have is "not good enough." What they believe manifests. What they have, no matter how good it is, will never be good enough, because that is what they believe. They believe they do not have what they need and they manifest a "not have" attitude for themselves.

I'm sure we all know someone who is always complaining. It would not matter if you gave them everything you had; including the shirt off your back; they would still be the same.

It is their attitude that is the problem. Until they are ready to acknowledge what they have, and be grateful for it, they will always be the same. We probably all have moments when we are not as appreciative as we should be. We might grumble about something, only to realise later that it was the best thing for us at the time. When we start to realise that what we are given, is exactly what we ask for, then it will change our attitude towards everything. An enlightened attitude will bring all that we desire to our very own homes.

The universe gives us everything, and we often fail to recognise this, and in so doing, we are negating it and pushing it away. Gratitude fills the heart. Resentment cannot live with gratitude. Gratitude is fulfilling by itself. Remember, we *do* live in an abundant universe! We should always remember to thank our guides and angels before we receive what we are asking for. This is the way the law works. We *expect* to receive it; therefore we thank them for it; knowing that it is already there for us on the next plane.

By being grateful for the small things we *do* have, we can change the very vibration of the law of life. Gratitude creates a vortex of energy around us, which brings everything to us that we could ever want. The unchanging law of giving and abundance that is Universal, will bring more to those who offer thanks and are grateful, many times over. There is no limit to what we can receive if we open ourselves to the eternal spirit of gratitude that is within us. When we fail to have gratitude for what we have, we fail to see the opportunities that are there for our growth. We also fail to see the need for gratitude in the evolution of our planet. When we are grateful for all that comes to us, we raise our vibrations, and that of the planet. Once we allow this consciousness to be a natural part of our daily lives, we are assisting in the earth's ascension in ways we cannot even imagine.

Our gratitude should be to the living earth itself, as it provides all our needs from the smallest seed to the air we breathe. Gratitude can change the whole way we see life. It gives us a power over our negative feelings, as it boosters up any feelings of resentment or depression we might have. When we begin our day with gratitude in our hearts, we allow all things we could ever desire to come to fulfilment in our lives: peace, love, joy and the light of true knowledge. As we find this light of knowledge, we become more open to the reality of the spiritual world that surrounds us.

Chapter 14

᠁

DOLPHIN AND WHALE
CONSCIOUSNESS

DOLPHINS HAVE NEVER BEEN KNOWN to harm man. Throughout the centuries stories have come down to us of dolphins guiding ships to shore. They have been known to intervene when a shark was attacking, butting them with their strong snouts, and sending them on their way. They have even carried a baby to safety from a catastrophic earthquake some years ago in Bangladesh. Dolphins have helped to assist retarded children, and have been known to heal injuries with their sonic cries.

People have psychically seen dolphins in Sedona in the United States, and some have been able to talk to them through telepathic means when they have been out in the sea. Dolphins seem to telepathically understand what we say to them. Their intelligence, and that of whales, is at least as great as man's, if not greater. They show us how to enjoy life by emanating our tactics in the water. They exhibit feats which show us how to enjoy life, and seem to live life to the full with the greatest delight. They could show us so much about how to live in joy.

Whales are large mammals of the same family as dolphins. They seem to understand man and are also capable of great feats. From intergalactic sources we are told that whales send messages to other planets which are heard in outer space. Their deep whale sounds, which sound like a loud bull-like roar, reverberate under the water and echo throughout the seas and the up into the hemisphere. They are of the same soul group as dolphins, and both groups have a mass consciousness, not individual consciousnesses like man does. That is, what happens to one dolphin or whale; is known to the rest, by telepathic means. This is why we find whales beached on the shore. There is a reason for this. They are here to awaken humanity and to bring to humankind, an awareness of a higher intelligence. They are awakening us to empathy and understanding, which opens our consciousness and spreads this quickening throughout humanity.

The consciousness of this planet is changing. The compassion that is aroused when dolphins and whales are beached is one prime example. Many more people are becoming aware of the need to support our planet and the life on our planet. There have been mass beachings of whales around the world, and people have been showing compassion and concern for these wonderful mammals, trying to assist their survival by keeping them alive until they can be dragged back to sea.

On the Internet, the following was theorised by Geologist, Jim Berkland:

> "A theory advanced by Geologist Jim Berkland, formerly with the U.S. Geological Survey, attributes the strandings to radical changes in the Earth's magnetic field just prior to earthquakes and in the general area of earthquakes. Berkland says when this occurs, it interferes with sea mammals' and even migratory birds' ability to navigate, which explains the mass beaching. He claims dogs and cats can also sense the disruptions, which explains elevated rates of runaway pets one to two days before earthquakes. Research on Earth's magnetic field and how it is affected by moving tectonic plates and earthquakes is ongoing.
>
> "There is evidence that active sonar leads to beaching. On some occasions whales have stranded shortly after military sonar was active in the area, suggesting a link."
>
> -Wikipedia, the free encyclopedia

"The overwhelming majority of the whales involved in sonar-associated beachings are Cuvier's Beaked Whales (Ziphius cavirostrus). This species strands frequently, but mass strandings are rare.

-Wikipedia, the free encyclopedia

Volunteers attempt to keep body temperatures of beached pilot whales from rising at Farewell Spit, New Zealand.

-Wikipedia, the free encyclopedia

What is actually happening is that the whales and dolphins are awakening our consciousness by being an instrument, giving their lives for the sake of humanity's awakening. Their time on this planet has been to assist man throughout the ages, and it is nearly over. The Star Trek IV where the Enterprise crew rescue a whale which is one of the few left on earth in the twentieth century is not far off the mark. There will be a gradual decrease of these wonderful mammals, until finally there are none left, because their greater purpose on this planet will have been fulfilled. They will have awakened humanity!

Chapter 15

OUR INTER-DIMENSIONAL
BROTHERS

T HE FACT THAT WE HAVE space brothers out there may be
the one thing which some will find so very hard to accept.
Surely man, in his ignorance, cannot really believe we are
the only intelligent life form in the whole of the universe? We have
been seeded, watched, and guided by our space brothers from the
beginning of the earth's formation!

There has, however, never been a time in earth's history,
when the interest in our little planet has been so great from an
intergalactic point of view. Because of the current cataclysmic
events happening on this planet, there is much interest in what
is now happening here from many other intelligence beings. We
most certainly *are not alone!*

Some information I received on the question of where we came
from and whether we really seeded from other planets, was:

> *Mankind is indeed seeded. He has far to go. Many of*
> *those upon the earth now are from the higher planets.*
> *Many star seeds have been born on earth to help uplift*
> *the races. Mankind is splitting again into those who have*
> *totally lost their way, that is, they are heavily immersed*
> *in materialism, and those who are more enlightened upon*
> *the planet. There will be great traumas as the two types*

clash. Mankind is about to be awakened. Much is being done in the heavenly realms to assist in this. We are ready and willing to help any who ask for our assistance. Sincerity of prayer is important. Likewise is willingness. You, mankind of earth, are destined to change. If you do not change, your destiny will be your own destruction. Other worlds before you have been destroyed. We are here to help, so this will not occur on this beautiful planet. Materialism is the thing which is the most threatening danger at the present time. Mankind must realise that his saving grace will come through his spiritual growth only.

I believe the majority of beings who are interacting with us at this time, are here to help us. Many are waiting 'in the wings' and watching for just such a chance. We are on the verge of a great happening, and those who helped seed us in the beginning are here to watch over and assist their earthly brothers in this time of earth's transition.

There is much written on the space beings and their work with this planet. They are here to help enlighten our planet and assist humanity in raising its vibrations from the heavy third dimension into a lighter vibration of fifth dimension. Humankind, we are told, is to be raised to a higher consciousness, and the time will come when we are able to be in full and total consciousness as we live here on the earth.

We will, in the near future, be allowed to join the Galactic Federation of Planets and travel to other planetary systems with those of like mind. But we will not be allowed to join, until we have proven we are a peaceful race. We will be given any and all technology we need to make this transition; but not until we have shown that we have evolved through love first. At that time, earth will be a planet where poverty has ceased, and earth people, as one, unite with other space brothers in peace.

The beings that helped seed this planet many millions of years ago are now returning, to look over the results of their handiwork, and readying to welcome home their 'families' to a greater degree of light and consciousness.

Because of the transition that the planet is undergoing, there is much curiosity from other life forms. Very few do not have the planet's or humanity's best interests at heart. Most are readying and preparing humanity to join the Galactic Federation in the near future.

The beings which have come to assist humanity have only good intentions. In fact they are here for the sole purpose of benefiting and assisting humankind. Those of the higher spiritual realms are in allegiance with the Galactic Federation and are assisting the planet. They have decreed that humankind is to be given the chance to redeem itself from the terrible disasters that have befallen it in the past ten thousand years. We have been given our day of grace. Our little planet is to be given great honour in the whole of our universe, and it is to become a beautiful star of light.

This may sound not readily believable, but there have been many who have spoken to these beings through telepathic means. Many are today channelling members of the Spiritual Hierarchy. There are also those from other planets who look very much like us, and can walk around our planet today and nobody would know they were any different. These beings however, are enlightened, and are in full consciousness of who they are. They are in a physical form as we are, but because they can heighten their vibrations to higher dimensions, they can, at will, also become invisible to our naked eye if they so choose. It is important to remember that they come in love. They come for no other purpose than to help humankind. They have developed far beyond our own limited ego based society, and have reached a point where their society is only for the benefit of serving others.

These interplanetary beings are in full consciousness. They are in both a physical third dimensional body and their light body. They can live for thousands of our years and do not age or die in the sense that we know death. They simply make a transition to a higher form when they leave their body. They come into life with full consciousness and are taught their soul-purpose for their lifetime from babies. They know from inception their life purpose.

They live in love and are in total harmony with the God-Source. They are one with the Will of the Creator.

This is where humanity is heading. This is what enlightenment is all about. Humanity is going on a roller-coaster ride, through turbulent times, in order to reach a higher state of consciousness which will eventually bring us into harmony, peace on earth, with all humanity. We will live for the purpose of serving and loving our brother/sister in all of humanity and understanding the connection we have with all life forms. We will be in greater harmony with the earth herself.

These times have been predicted for aeons. They are upon us now. But first we have to face the tribulations which we have been seeing signs of in the past few decades. Our planet is about to enter a new era, one in which souls will no longer be allowed to enter the earth if they are of a negative vibration. The Earth herself is truly awakening and a new dawn is upon us.

Chapter 16

THE DAYS TO COME . . .

W
E ARE NOW SEEING MUCH of the changing times. There are even more turbulent times ahead, however don't lose heart. To be forewarned is to be forearmed. Remember that change and destruction has to take place in order for new constructions to appear.

I was told:

We welcome you on this your New Year Day in your concept of time. We do not have time as you do, as everything exists in the now.

There are indeed changes happening in your world which have greater ramifications. The weather is a sign of these changes. Mankind is being made aware of these changes through the pattern of your weather. The earth herself is being altered and man's conception of his home planet is about to change. There is naught to fear. All change is for a wider purpose. Be prepared to change self as these changes happen around you. All is in accord with Divine Law. The seasons are only one sign of the great shift which is to occur. Be prepared to accept whatever comes in each new day. The time for taking anything for granted is over. Each new moment has a different thing to offer you. Be prepared to accept each change as it occurs. There is nothing frightening or fearful in this—it is just different from what you may have anticipated in times past. You must realise that you cannot live in your past any more.

Only by going within and accepting what is in your now time will you find peace. Past and future will no longer have the hold over you that they once did. Live in the moment and be joy-filled. There is naught to fear. Be happy . . .

The more enlightened we are about our future and what to expect, the more we will be able to be in harmony as these things happen. We are children of the one Creator and as such we have opportunities to witness one of the greatest changes this planet has seen. Remember we are eternal. Nothing can harm us. If we do leave our physical bodies we only make the transition, we do not die. Love is eternal. Only love can be taken with us. We can never lose that which we never had in the first place. We are literally "embodiments of love". If we become enlightened through understanding and compassion, before we make this transition, we have served our life's purpose. We will have begun to see the changes which will herald our new world!

Many of us, like my husband, for example are afraid to look into the future for fear of what they will see. When I asked divine guidance about this the answer was as follows:

Your man is afraid to look to the future. He has much fear still within him. The years will unfold for him in good time. If each moment is made to count, the outcome will not be important, for you will be living in your higher consciousness and time as you know it, will cease to be the same. One day you will emerge from your bed of sleep and say: "Has two years of time really passed? It seems like only yesterday!"

When you are fully immersed in your now moment there is no past or present. All is at that moment—and that, my child is how life was always meant to be. Your good man will see the future as a time for him to rest, but indeed he will not rest. His fear of the future will push him on to further activities and he will not get his chance to look back to the times past and say "Where has the time gone?" for indeed he will be living his past, present, and future in the one moment.

Life is an ongoing cycle and nothing that exists is permanent, yet at the same time, no lesson learned is ever lost. You will see self in the future and wonder if you ever were the being you see now. Your concept of time is changing so fast even those upon your plane called scientists, are indeed investigating this, your concept of time.

Live in the present moment and be joyful. The future will unfold as it is meant to be.

All of our reactions are caused by our past connection to something. If we live in the present, there is no guilt of the past, no fear for the future, there is just now! That is how this world will be in the days to come. We are coming into an Age when all will be living in the now. So many people these days have instant amnesia. They can't remember what they were going to do or say. They forget things that they did yesterday. The effect is throughout all generations. It is not just the elderly or middle-aged people who are having this problem. Even my younger daughter was forgetting things that she never once would have forgotten.

Our earth is moving into another dimension, literally! We are finding ourselves more and more, living only in the present. The past is slipping away, as memories are fading. We will have no need to carry extra baggage into the new Age. Our memories will be transmuted through love and will become part of our now. Because of the changes happening to us, we will be more open psychically to contacting those we have loved and lost through physical death. We will have moved our consciousness into a higher dimension.

Some of the changes are already happening. The earth herself is rebelling against the mistreatment over the last few centuries of abuse and rape by humankind. She is cracking as her belly is opened and earthquakes tremble, to rid her of the poisons humanity has treated her with. She is spewing forth her volcanoes, raging her seas and sending her winds to parch the earth and her rains to flood the plains, causing mudslides and creating much havoc.

We are told also that our bodies are changing. This could explain why so many are suffering from illnesses including so many different allergies that are emerging, especially among the children. Influenza-like symptoms, viruses and gastric problems are also prevalent. Our bodies are being cleansed of all toxins and this is one of the ways to clear them. Our bodies know what they need. They are cleansing themselves to take in more and more of their light bodies.

We will see again an increase in the fall of the economic markets world-wide. The banks will fall as will the stock market and the larger insurance companies. Many will be trying to survive as more and more people become jobless. This has been happening now for a decade or more. It will be crucial times which will call for much strength from our inner sources. People who are not balanced will become further imbalanced as they begin to turn to crime in order to survive. Mechanical equipment will start to fail and there will be numerous accidents, both in the air and on the ground.

The earth, which has suffered so much abuse, will release some of the radioactive waste buried deep within her bowels. These leaks have already begun to happen and worse could be waiting, if humanity does not wake up to the hurt being caused by the nuclear wastes and weapons.

Our brothers from space will land among us and converse with many. They will be the saving grace for humanity, as people begin to become disheartened and angry with the governments, and question their long kept secrets, and their own religions. These beings will assist us by showing us how we can overcome our difficulties through brotherly love to each other. More people will find their psychic powers opened as they become more attuned with their higher sources.

Again I was advised to live in the moment:

Live in the now moment and do not let thoughts of past worry you. You are a multidimensional being, and the thoughts you have are not yours alone, but belong to the many beings that are also part of you. Your multidimensional selves are coming to the point where freedom is in sight for them all. You are about to embark on a wonderful journey to freedom. Be happy. This time is not far off. Let each day bring you more joy. Live in that joy and let not past worries intervene. There is much light about you. Let it shine for the world needs it now more than ever. Those things which are brought to the light are brought to be healed. Have no fear that harm will come to any. These things are necessary for healing of situations. Simply allow all things to come to the light. Be steady in your thoughts.

Send your loving thoughts to everyone you feel has need of them, for we can affect their arrival. Thoughts are real. Do not be deceived that they are not. Your loving thoughts will find their target. Pray often. There is hope for every situation. Believe that all is possible through the love of the Creator. These thoughts we leave with you . . .

The coming days, once the worst is over, will be a time of rejoicing. We will literally see the great prophecies fulfilled, as the "lamb lays down with the lion". Cattle will not be afraid of losing their lives any longer, as the new day dawns. Animals of all species will commune in families and live in peace again, as it was in the beginning. There will be a greater consciousness among humankind and we will be enlightened by the growing light within.

We are advised to face our ailments with understanding and acceptance as these changes occur.

Many are finding ailments today. Be of good cheer. Happier times are ahead. We know you are going through some trialing times at the moment but they won't last. Learn your lesson well and these times will pass more quickly. I am your guiding light. Fear not.

> *These times are for your growth. Learn well and these lessons will become lessons of joy. Let not your heart be troubled. Take all things in your stride and one day they will be looked upon as the greatest treasures life could give you. These things are in themselves unpolished jewels to be transformed into the most dazzling beauty you could ever imagine. These lights of beauty are just waiting to be revealed to you. The promises of the future go with you.*
>
> *Walk in light and be glad . . . We love you.*

We, as humanity, are becoming fully consciousness beings, and will be able to communicate with others in higher dimensions. There will be no barriers to what we can do. We will learn to use antigravity as a means to transport ourselves. We will have laws but they will be good laws. They will be in alignment with the Higher Will.

Once we become aware enough of ourselves as divine beings, and treat everyone else as if they were divine also, we will find crime and greed disappear. There will be no need for insecurities and fears. The last vestiges of these are being played out in our world right now. Their time is short dear reader. Be hopeful and joyful. Our promised thousand years of peace *is* coming! Our days will be longer upon this planet as peace envelopes the whole of humanity and lower life forms as well. We will raise our vibrations to a higher dimension and will live to see this transition of our beautiful planet within our lifetimes!

Take heart all who read. Peace is just around the corner. Those who are aware enough to understand these words will be the ones to be the leaders and the councillors in the days to come. Know that *you* are Divine Essence. You are love. You are as much a part of God as anyone else. All have equal claim to that right.

Enlightenment comes through understanding. Enlightenment comes through non-judgement and unconditional love. Enlightenment comes through "feeling the daily daggers of relentless steel and keeping on living". Enlightenment is raising our consciousness towards our Higher Self, or greater light.

Enlightenment is reaching our arms out to our fellowman in compassion and concern. Enlightenment is expressing the living truth in each moment we walk the path of light, in whatever our jobs are, or whatever course our lives take.

The promises for our future are embodied in the following song. It was sung to the tune of Amazing Grace by Silarra, one of the extraterrestrial walk-ins who have come to help our planet:

> *Amazing grace, compassion and truth*
> *Aqua star—ship of blue light.*
> *We have come to Earth to live its dream:*
> *A heaven of pure delight!*
>
> *We share our forces here with you*
> *Of inside wisdom and love.*
> *We live here upon this plane*
> *As we do in the ships above.*
>
> *There are more than twelve thousand groups of twelve*
> *We have gathered from afar.*
> *We have come to fill the Earth with light,*
> *To fulfil her birth as a star.*
>
> *We speak to you of Heaven on Earth*
> *It's within if you'll just allow.*
> *Don't hesitate, your Spirit calls—*
> *Wake up—the time is now!*

Afterword

THIS BOOK WAS ORIGINALLY WRITTEN some years ago. Since that time, we, as a human race, have already implemented many of the changes to our consciousness on our journey toward enlightenment.

We have become more aware of our individuality; we have become more aware of our experiences of being part of the whole; and we are more in tune with what is important as a race of human beings on this, our planet earth.

The awareness of looking after our planet is very evident in demonstrations; such as world-wide memorials to the memory of the atomic destruction at Hiroshima. People are realising that we *have to be aware* not to destroy our planet. Environment issues are now being brought to the fore by institutions such as Greenpeace; and many others are warning us about climate change, and how carbon emissions are effecting the our atmosphere. This is a small sampling of how we are now becoming aware of our environment and how important it is for us to live *with* the planet and not destroy it. The earth is a living being!

Changes are happening to us individually too. Many more are listening to their inner voice and finding they need to work from home rather than from a place of employment where they were in a regular nine to five job. Many more are settling for casual employment rather than permanent, and are free to pursue their own interests in their free time.

Life is to be *lived;* to the fullest extent.

We are here for such a short time in the journey of our souls. We are here to live in the *now!* We always have been meant to experience life and to find love in every situation we find ourselves, and always meant to live in the now moment. What happened in the past or will happen in the future is irrelevant. All is now. Spreading love from our centre will change the world. Love is the only hope for humanity.

Let us begin now to experience the love that we really are.

Chris Hamilton
2013

BIBLIOGRAPHY

ANDERSON, Jane—Dream it: Do it!

AZENA—St. Germain—Earth's Birth Changes.

BARTHOLOMEW—Planetary Brother

BRAMLEY, William—The Gods of Eden.

BURNHAM, Sophy—A Book of Angels.

CALDECOTT, Moyra—Guardians of the Tall Stones—The Sacred Stones Trilogy

CANON, Delores—Jesus and The Essenes. Fresh insights into Christ's Ministry and the Dead Sea Scrolls.

CANNON, Dolores—Keepers of the Garden

CAREY, Ken—Starseed The Third Millennium. Living in the Posthistoric World

CAYCE, Edgar—Dreams: Your Magic Mirror

CHANEY, Earlyne—The Madonna and the Coming Light.

CHOPRA, Deepak—The Return of Merlin.

CHOPRA, Deepak—The Way of the Wizard.

CLOW, Barbara Hand—Heart of the Cristos. Starseeding from the Pleiades

CLOW, Barbara Hand—The Pleiadian Agenda

COHEN, Alan—The Dragon Doesn't Live Here Anymore.

DANNELLEY, Richard—Sedona UFO Connection and Planetary Ascension Guide

DAWSON, Michael—Healing the Cause—A Path of Forgiveness

DONGO, Tom—The Quest. The Mysteries of Sedona Book III

DYER, Dr Wayne—Gifts from Eykis

ENSOR, Kenny—Manual for advancing souls

ENSOR, Kenny—This is my world

ESSENE, Virginia & NIDLE, Sheldon—You are Becoming a Galactic Human

ESSENE, Virginia & VALENTIN, Ann—Cosmic Revelation

FEARHEILEY, Don.—Angels Among Us.

GAWAIN, Shakti—Creative Visualization.

GAWAIN, Shakti—The Path of Transformation.

GAWAIN, Shakti—Return to the Garden.

GOLDEN Star Alliance—I'm O.K. I'm Just Mutating!

GREAVES, Helen—Testimony of Light

GREAVES, Helen—The Wheel of Eternity

GRISCOM, Chris—Time is an Illusion.

HAY, Louise L.—The Power is Within You.

HILL, Dawn.—With a Little Help from my Friends.

HOLBECHE, Soozi—Awakening to Change. A guide to self—empowerment in the new millennium

HOLMSTROM, John—When Prayers Are Answered.

JEFFERS, Susan.—Feel The Fear And Do It Anyway.

KING, Jani—The P'Taah Tapes. An Act of Faith.

KING, Jani—The P'Taah Tapes. Transformation of the Species

KIRKWOOD, Anni—Mary's Message to the World

KLEIN, Eric—The Crystal Stair. A Guide to the Ascension

KRISHNAMURTI—On Nature and the Environment

LAKE, Gina—The Extraterrestrial Vision.

LIND, Ingrid—The Spiritual Teachings of White Eagle

LITCHFIELD, Beverley—On Wings Unfolded. A journey towards the light

LUPPI, Diana—E.T. 101 The Cosmic Instruction Manual.

MACLAINE, Shirley—Out on a Limb.

MANI-ZEHAR, Channelled by Xletar—Awaken Star Seeds. Who are You? Why are you here?

MARCINIAK, Barbara—Bringers of the Dawn, Teachings from the Pleiadians

MARCINIAK, Barbara—Earth. Pleiadian Keys to the Living Library

MILLER, Carolyn Ph.D.—Creating Miracles. Understanding the Experience of Divine Intervention.

MILLMAN, Dan.—Sacred Journey of the Peaceful Warrior

MONTGOMERY, Ruth—Strangers Among Us.

MONTGOMERY, Ruth with GARLAND, Ruth—Herald of The New Age.

MORSE, Dr Melvin—Parting Visions. An Exploration of Pre-Death Psychic and Spiritual Experiences

MURPHET, Howard—Invitation to Glory.

O'BRIEN, Stephen—Visions of Another World

PAINE, Wingate—The Book of Surrender. A Journey to Self-Awareness Inspired by the Words of Emmanuel

PECK, M. Scott—The Road Less Travelled.

PETERSON, Jean—Oneness Remembered. By Sananda Jesus the Christ

QUILLER, Peter & DAVIS, Courtney—Merlin Awakes. Revelations and Truths for a New Age

RAIN, Mary Summer—Daybreak The Dawning Ember

RAIN, Mary Summer—Phoenix Rising.

RIDALL, Kathryn Ph.D.—Channeling. How to Reach Out to your Spirit Guides.

RAMANDA, Azena & HEARTSONG, Claire—St Germain. Twin Souls & Soulmates

RAMPA, T. Lobsang—The Hermit

RANDALL, Neville—Life After Death.

REDFIELD, James—The Celestine Prophecy

REPPEL, Erica—The Journey Home

ROADS, Michael J.—Journey Into Nature.

ROBERTS, Jane—Seth Speaks

ROGERS, Elizabeth Jean—Create Your Own Joy. A Guide for Transforming your Life.

ROMAN, Sanaya & PACKER, Duane—Opening to Channel. How to Connect with your Guide.

SANDYS, Cynthia—The Awakening Letters Volume Two

SCHLEMMER, Phyllis & JENKINS, Palden—The Only Planet of Choice.

SCHLOTTERBECK, Karl—Living your Past Lives: The Psychology of Past-Life Regression.

SCOLASTICO, Ron, Ph.D.—The Earth Adventure. Your Soul's Journey through Physical Reality

SEDONA Vortex Guide Book

SMITH, Robert C.—In the Presence of Angels.

SOLARA—Invoking your Celestial Guardians.

STICHIN, Zecharia—When Time Began

TAYLOR, Terry Lynn—Messengers of Light. The Angels' Guide to Spiritual Growth

THE WISDOM OF RAMALA

TUELLA—On Earth Assignment

TUIETA—Conclave: 5th Meeting

TUIETA—El Morya. Talks with the Masters.

TUIETA—Letters from Home Vol. 1

TUIETA—Letters from Home Vol. 11

ULLMAN, Montague M.D. & ZIMMERMAN, Nan—Working with Dreams.

WHITFIELD, Charles M.D.—Boundaries and Relationships.

WILSON, A.N.—Jesus.

WYLLIE, Timothy—Dolphins ETs & Angels

WYLLIE, Timothy—Dolphins Telepathy & Underwater Birthing

YARBRO, Chelsea Quinn—Messages from Michael